A Short History of Trans Misogyny

A Short History
of Trans Misogyny

Jules Gill-Peterson

VERSO
London • New York

First published by Verso 2024
© Jules Gill-Peterson 2024

1 3 5 7 9 10 8 6 4 2

Verso
UK: 6 Meard Street, London W1F 0EG
US: 388 Atlantic Avenue, Brooklyn, NY 11217
versobooks.com

Verso is the imprint of New Left Books

ISBN-13: 978-1-80429-156-6
ISBN-13: 978-1-80429-161-0 (UK EBK)
ISBN-13: 978-1-80429-162-7 (US EBK)

British Library Cataloguing in Publication Data
A catalogue record for this book is available from the British Library

Library of Congress Cataloging-in-Publication Data

Names: Gill-Peterson, Jules, author.
Title: A short history of trans misogyny / Jules Gill-Peterson.
Description: London ; New York : Verso, 2024. | Includes bibliographical
   references and index.
Identifiers: LCCN 2023036325 (print) | LCCN 2023036326 (ebook) | ISBN
   9781804291566 (hardback) | ISBN 9781804291627 (ebook)
Subjects: LCSH: Transmisogyny. | Transgender women—Violence against.
Classification: LCC HQ77.96 .G55 2024 (print) | LCC HQ77.96 (ebook) | DDC
   306.76/8082—dc23/eng/20230815
LC record available at https://lccn.loc.gov/2023036325
LC ebook record available at https://lccn.loc.gov/2023036326

Typeset in Sabon by MJ & N Gavan, Truro, Cornwall
Printed and bound by CPI Group (UK) Ltd, Croydon CR0 4YY

Contents

Preface

"Trans misogyny" refers to the targeted devaluation of both trans femininity and people perceived to be trans feminine, regardless of how they understand themselves. While it can manifest as a system of beliefs, trans misogyny also structures the material world through disparate life outcomes and a suite of characteristically punitive regimes. As an exercise of interpersonal or state violence, trans misogyny operates through the logic of the preemptive strike. It *trans-feminizes* its targets without their assent, usually by sexualizing their presumptive femininity as if it were an expression of male aggression. This process of misrecognition and projection construes its targets as inherently threatening. The threat label, in turn, justifies aggression or punishment rationalized after the fact as a legitimate response to having been victimized—a self-interested playbook if there ever was one. Whoever pursues trans misogyny enjoys the rare privilege of being at once the victim *and* the judge, jury, and executioner. The transgression prompting this full-court press can be as mundane as walking down the street, or a moral panic as overinflated as the putative end of Western civilization. Regardless, the passive presence of a trans-feminized person is almost always the solipsistic pretense for striking first. Trans misogyny attacks the very *existence* of trans femininity in attacking real people.

Trans misogyny is both highly discerning, isolating its targets from the rest of the social world, and wildly impersonal, recruiting elements of homophobia and conventional misogyny to its cause. It also tends to manifest through local idioms of racism and class antagonism. This book outlines those characteristics and mechanics in greater detail, tracing some of their key historical points of emergence over the past two hundred years. Throughout, I insist on trans misogyny as the infrastructure of the shared world to release the pressure to sort human worth through identity and social position. While each day seems to bring new taxonomies for assigning value to would-be gender identities, sex classes, or variously privileged and oppressed people, I offer this book as a materialist case for leaving such losing games behind. My first axiom is that trans misogyny is too ubiquitous to make such lofty distinctions. It sticks to and gums up nearly everything concerning sex, gender, sexuality, race, and class. I don't believe in sorting people's relative degrees of guilt or victimhood through what kind of person they are because that is precisely what trans misogyny does. Worse, doing so makes for resentful, purity-obsessed solutions to social inequities. In truth, everyone is implicated in and shaped by trans misogyny. There is no one who is purely *affected* by it to the point of living in a state of total victimization, just as there is no one who lives entirely *exempt* from its machinations. There is no perfect language to be discovered, or invented, to solve the problem of trans misogyny by labeling its proper perpetrator and victim. Nor is anyone's degree of safety or harm determined or *assigned* in any final way, whether at birth or through the allegory of *socialization*. There are, likewise, no biologically static, inherent attributes from which to extrapolate anyone's deservingness of recognition, freedom, or quality of life, let alone their fantasized inherent criminality or power. Every attempt to legislate how the world ought to be by pretending to innocently describe its normative rules will fail to deliver, as all idealizations do in their overconfidence. This book is critical in its procedures of analysis, but it is also, crucially, empiricist in its reliance on the evidence of the past.

The present era of screeching moral panic, frothing authoritarianism, and endless crisis in the capitalist system has been unkind to us all. Lately I've reflected on how brittle I've become, at least by some measures. When the stakes are set so permanently high as life or death, catastrophe or salvation, it's difficult to front the cost of vulnerability, including the vulnerability needed to inhabit uncertainty or tender provisional thoughts. It feels immensely difficult to risk being wrong today, especially in public, and I'm not immune. I've found myself saying less outside of the labored prose of my research and scholarship, which builds in a million opportunities to choose my words carefully. (This book is one example of that, to be sure.) The debate club of what remains of the public sphere is a surreal nightmare. For every right-wing pundit or liberal launderer of extremism whose vitriol splatters on the windshield of my public-facing self, there's the symmetrical rudeness and aggression of people I don't know, but who seem otherwise to be in the struggle with me. Moral panics are not restricted to anti-trans projects. There are queer moral panics and even trans moral panics directed intramurally—at ourselves, by ourselves. And though they hurt differently because they are seldom backed by the overwhelming force of the state, they do wound in a manner the people explicitly dedicated to the fool's errand of my eradication cannot. Frustrated and exhausted by pervasive bad faith, lately I've found myself saying less that I'm not absolutely sure of. And I'm not talking about practicing boundaries, or being opaque to reserve some interiority as a writer—which we all might want to do. I mean something that mixes self-censorship through silence with the arterial hardening that comes from a lifetime of being let down, by racism as much as by homophobia and trans misogyny.

Trans misogyny is highly compatible with right-wing authoritarian politics because it aims to preserve, or entrench, existing social hierarchies through the production of an imagined threat from those with the least demonstrated power, demanding violence to put them down. However, it would be a mistake to think this means liberal or left politics are immune, or even less amenable, to wielding its power. Trans misogyny is a rare point of consensus across any proverbial spectrum, be it of politics, identity, or desire. I hope that the meticulous approach of this book, which aims to provide overwhelming evidence as a resource in your hands, also moves you in a different way. If you, like me, feel a little brittle, uncertain of how to break the relentless march of the wretched order of things, then perhaps defending your own goodness, even through learning or politicking, is not the most urgent task. Trans misogyny functions less as anyone's personal failure than something like the weather. Relinquishing the drive to seek political clarity in the goodness, or badness, of your demography might yield far bigger rewards. What awaits is a certain *un*-learning, a task for which this book might be one humble guide.

Jules Gill-Peterson
September 14, 2022

Introduction

Femmes against Trans

We are living in the global era of *trans*, a shortened or prefixal version of the word *transgender*. As an umbrella promoted by the global North, *trans* is a hyper-inclusive category under which a constellation of gender identities and styles are meant to find their home. As a prefix, *trans-* is also a kind of boundary-crossing energy, a refusal to be contained by binaries, and attachable to nearly anything: not just people around the world in countless cultures and languages, but also animals, molecules of animate matter, or digital technology.[1] *Trans* is caught between describing a small minority of people and naming something hyper-modern about how the world works. But *trans*, as the inheritor of *transgender*, is also uniquely premised on the distortion and domestication of trans femininity. Prefixal trans politics promise a queer utopia of gender in which everyone else is set free by getting rid of a backward trans womanhood. This is an origin story that is rarely told.

The word *transgender* rose to popularity in the 1990s in two related but distinct births. The first was a largely white activist world in the San Francisco Bay Area, where people long involved in queer organizing began to rally around *transgender* as a nonmedical, avowedly political category for trespassing the enforced boundaries of gender. Swaths of people in the United States who had previously traveled under disparate and even incompatible signs were suddenly lumped together under a single umbrella, including transvestites, drag queens, cross-dressers, street queens, hair fairies, butches, studs, bois, faggots, femmes, gender fluid and genderfuck people, and transsexuals. This activist milieu produced radical and intersectional definitions of transgender as a sort of strategic coalition of the gender precariat, like Leslie Feinberg's influential 1992 pamphlet *Transgender Liberation: A Movement Whose Time Has Come*.[2] But the far bigger shadow cast by *transgender* came through its second birth in the well-funded NGO industrial complex. There, *transgender* was institutionalized by social service organizations working in US cities and was swiftly adopted for parallel international development work across the global South. For organizations doing safer-sex outreach work, HIV/AIDS care, and harm reduction, *transgender* carried the same definition it had for activists, at least on the surface. David Valentine, an anthropologist who studied the process firsthand in New York City, observed that these organizations imagined *transgender* in the late 1990s as "a *collective* category of identity which incorporates a diverse array of male- and female-bodied gender variant people who had previously been understood as distinct kinds of person."[3]

The problem, as Valentine saw most strikingly in his fieldwork with sex workers, was that few of the femmes being recategorized as transgender used the word to describe themselves. As social service organizations, charities, healthcare providers, and local bureaucracies began identifying street girls and sex workers under the transgender umbrella, they actively dismissed these women's understanding of themselves to include them in philanthropic projects. The biggest sticking point was femmes' use of the term *gay*. Valentine noticed that for NGOs, "transgender identification" was, above all, "to be explicitly and fundamentally different in origin and being from homosexual identification."[4] Calling poor street sex workers transgender was meant to distinguish them from gay people, but the distinction was imposed from the outside. As a result, the femmes on the street became even more illegible than they had been before. *Transgender* arrived for many girls on the street not as an activist cry but as an institutional word to abstractly separate gender identity from sexual orientation. By refusing to ratify that separation, these largely poor trans women of color were cast as backward, suffering from an "outmoded" belief system. Since then, the tendency to frame anyone who refuses to separate gender from sexuality as anachronistic has migrated to the global South, further entrenching the white, middle-class, Western model of gender identity as the hallmark of trans modernity. *Transgender*'s great accomplishment has thus been to disavow the very people it claims to urgently represent: poor women of color.

Around the same time Valentine was doing fieldwork in New York City's Meatpacking District, a season 3 episode of *Sex and the City* (2000) followed Samantha (Kim Cattrall) moving into a $7,000-a-month loft in the neighborhood. In now-infamous scenes, Samantha confronts a trio of Black trans women whose sex work is driving her to bourgeois tears. "I didn't pay a fortune to live in a neighborhood that's trendy by day and tranny by night," she exclaims to her friends during the show's iconic lunch scene. Samantha first tries to resolve the issue by complimenting the women's looks and asking if they would kindly move to another block. Carrie Bradshaw (Sarah Jessica Parker) chimes in as narrator to add that "Samantha always knew how to get her way with men, even if they were half women." But when the girls return and interrupt an orgasm with her boyfriend, Samantha flings open her bedroom window, screams, "Shut up you bitches, I called the cops!" and hurls a pot of water onto one of them. "I am a tax-paying citizen and a member of the Young Women's Business Association. I don't have to put up with this," she rants to herself. A police car then appears on the street and Samantha watches, triumphantly, as the Black trans women move on. At the end of the episode, feeling remorseful, Samantha hosts a rooftop party with the girls, befriending them once and for all—though not without getting in several more cringeworthy barbs.[5]

The episode, fans admit, hasn't aged well over the past twenty years.[6] As the documentary *Disclosure* (2020) might put it, the conventions of representing trans people have since traveled the so-called trans tipping point, in that framing Black trans women and sex workers as the butts of crude jokes colludes with their social death.[7] But perversely, the scene underlines how plainly *Sex and the City* offers a characteristically anti-Black form of trans misogyny. Samantha's dehumanization of the girls working her block is not the organ of a moral campaign against sex work or a philosophical crisis in the category of womanhood. It has to do quite simply with her status as a gentrifier. She wants the Meatpacking District policed and emptied of Black trans women because she pays exorbitant rent for her apartment. And she wants the privacy of her home to facilitate pleasurable straight sex with her boyfriend, which requires that it be separate from the public, transactional economy of sex work. There is nothing deliberately veiled in Samantha's actions or beliefs; they are explicit defenses of a bourgeois white woman. To purify the Meatpacking District and Samantha's home, the girls on the street must be evicted. Rewatching it today, viewers might find the episode remains oddly unambiguous about the gentrifying work of the global trans era.

Twenty years later, the world is hardly shy about discussing violence against trans women, though the cosmopolitan pendulum has swung from Samantha making jokes about that violence to raising awareness about it. In fact, violence is like the currency through which trans women circulate. In the public's mind, Black trans women like those portrayed on *Sex and the City* are tied to a powerful spectacle of harassment, sexual assault, policing, physical violence, and murder. And there is no shortage of voices demanding that everyone pay even more attention to that violence, as if beholding it is the key to its remedy. But in the constant repetition of scenes of violence, one frighteningly basic question seems never to be answered: Why does it happen?

Advocacy and domestic violence organizations rarely track violence against trans women as a stand-alone category, preferring to place it under a general "transgender" or "LGBT" heading. Yet they also describe the scope of that violence variously as a "plague," or an "epidemic" of "staggering" or "shocking" ubiquity.[8] And they contend that the rate of violence against trans women seems to be going up, especially for Black trans women and trans women of color.[9] Yet none of these organizations provide an explanation for *why* trans women are harassed, assaulted, and killed at such alarming or exceptional rates, or what makes the rate change. It's as if the answer is too self-evident and disturbing to entertain: some trans women are so widely reviled that they are uniquely killable.

Killing trans women is horrifying regardless of its motive. But the absence of causal explanations for such violence is tied to some strange prescriptions from advocacy groups. The National Center for Transgender Equality, for example, advocates the prosecution of violence against trans women of color in the US as hate crimes, even though hate crime statutes are, paradoxically, mostly used to criminalize people of color.[10] Lambda Legal, another civil rights organization, admits that police are rarely helpful in investigating this kind of violence, being themselves a significant source of harm to trans women.[11] Although the Human Rights Campaign notes that the causes of violence against trans women are too complicated for a single explanation (they call it a "culture of violence"), Tori Cooper, HRC's director of community engagement for its Transgender Justice Initiative, told *Time* magazine in 2021 that "we need to make sure that folks who commit hate crimes are prosecuted accordingly."[12]

5

The concept of hate crimes grafts a vague notion of trans-phobic "bias" onto a prefabricated explanation for violence: it happens because it's committed by criminals.[13] This premise has proven to be exceptionally weak in the face of the "trans panic" defense, which exonerates those who are brought to trial or reduces their sentences for attacking or killing trans women. In fact, the trans panic defense is so resilient that it has even survived being banned. In 2002, seventeen-year-old Gwen Araujo was beaten and strangled to death by four men in Newark, California. At trial, the defense claimed that the men only killed Araujo in the "heat of passion" after discovering her "biological sex." That characterization of events seems to have been untrue. Some of the defendants seemingly first had sex with Araujo *several days* before they killed her, meaning they could hardly have lost their sanity in the heat of the moment. But the claim that Araujo's body had so provoked them that they were justified in killing her overwhelmed the facts of the case. The jury deadlocked, leading to a mistrial. Two of the men were found guilty of second-degree murder at a second trial, while another remained the subject of a jury deadlock. The success of the trans panic defense in muddying the prosecu-tion led to a burst of organizing around violence against trans women and trans women of color like Araujo, and in response, California passed a law banning the trans panic defense (along with the "gay panic" defense).[14]

Yet only five years later, downstate in Oxnard, Brand McInerny shot his fifteen-year-old classmate Latisha King in the back of the head at point blank range, in full view of students and their teacher. McInerny had brought the gun from home, and the trial emphasized that he killed King not long after she had asked him to be her valentine. The murder of a Black trans girl in junior high was narrated as a case of unrequited love— a story that allowed everyone involved to avoid King's girl-hood. At trial, she was referred to by her birth name only, with male pronouns, and was repeatedly described as a gay boy. She was treated this way despite testimony that it was watching King type her name, Latisha, on a classroom computer that had triggered McInerney to pull the gun.[15]

"Much of what happened at this trial hinged on confusion between gender identity and sexual orientation," explains feminist scholar Gayle Salamon in her book examining the case. The evidence presented to explain why McInerney killed King included the clothing she wore to school, the way she walked down the hallway, and the tone of voice she used in speaking to him, all which were interpreted as sexual harassment of McInerney. King was misgendered over and over as male to reframe her as inherently aggressive toward a straight white boy—inferences that made tactically unspoken use of her Blackness and trans femininity as certification. At trial, it was suddenly as if King had somehow pushed McInerney to kill her, to the point that he was not responsible for bringing a gun to school, pointing it at her, and pulling the trigger. This "submerged logic" on the defense's part, as Salamon puts it, worked without any evidence precisely because Latisha's "feminine gender was already a panic-inducing provocation" to everyone in the courtroom, even after her death. McInerney's extreme violence—executing her in front of their class—became coldly rational "by characterizing non-normative gender as itself a violent act of aggression … reading the expression of gender identity *as itself a sexual act*."[16]

As with Araujo's killers, McInerney's plea deal reduced the charges to second-degree murder;[17] and state prosecutors failed to land a hate crime charge against him. Even though the trans panic defense was by then illegal in California, it was successfully employed through the conflation of trans femininity and homosexuality.

Even if the concept of hate crimes could outwit illegal trans panic defenses, calls to imprison the killers of trans women and girls, or to stick them with longer sentences, have nothing to do with justice. On the contrary, the failure of these trials to secure higher-level convictions is not a problem worth solving. Nor would justice have been achieved if the court had recognized that Latisha was a girl. The point is that the original violence of assault or murder is in fact extended through legal proceedings, serving as a retrospective guarantee. The misgendering of trans femininity as male sexual aggression, particularly when racist fantasies about Black and Brown sexuality are encoded in the conflation, allows people to respond to trans femininity with as much preemptive violence as they desire. All they have to do is claim panic after the fact.

The *panic* in trans panic has generated a mostly psychological analysis. Writer and activist Julia Serano, who helpfully distinguishes trans misogyny's characteristic sexism from a generic notion of transphobia, points out that violence against trans women is generally justified as appropriate punishment for "deception." Through the hypersexualization of trans femininity, trans women are seen as inviting not just sexual interest but any violence required to reassert straight men's position over them in the social hierarchy. The sexualization of trans women, ironically, threatens men by association, like a boomerang of desire. "Behind every accusation of deception lies an unchallenged assumption," Serano explains, "that no male in his right mind could ever be attracted to someone who was feminine, yet physically male."[18]

The philosopher Talia Mae Bettcher emphasizes that this dynamic creates a situation no trans woman can successfully navigate. The killing of trans women by men is often explained as stemming from a failure to disclose being trans. But that "failure"—and the subsequent moment of "discovery"—seems just as often to be a lie invented after the fact to mitigate consequences, as it was at the trial of Araujo's killers. The choice whether or not to disclose isn't decisive, because trans women lack control over how they are perceived in everyday life. "There is an important difference between coming out as a 'transgender woman' and as 'really a man disguised as a woman,'" Bettcher explains. "Yet it is often the latter that does much of the work in transphobic violence," regardless of how trans women present themselves, or whether they pass.[19] This is why trans women who pass so well that men don't initially know they are trans are actually more endangered by passing, rather than enjoying a privilege. Thus, the victim-blaming of trans women has little to do with what they say or how they act. The trope of deception is a blanket projection of a culture that sheds accountability onto the women targeted by violence.

Like many trans feminists, Serano and Bettcher treat violence against trans women as an important subset of misogynist violence in general. But the psychological analysis runs out of steam there. As the philosopher Kate Manne explains, psychological explanations convert misogyny into "a property of individual agents (typically, although not necessarily men) who are prone to feel hatred, hostility, or other similar emotions towards any and every woman, or at least women generally, simply because they are women." But there are few people who fit such an extreme definition. Misogyny is not only pure or abstract woman-hating; in practice it fixes itself to women forced to live at the bottom of other social hierarchies, like race and class, that already overexpose them to violence. Misogyny selects people like trans women based on compounding factors that make it easier to victim-blame them and escape accountability.[20] (Misogyny also promises protection to women who pledge their allegiance to misogynist causes, which partly explains why many anti-trans feminists, such as some right-wing women, are content to align with misogynist men in the dehumanization of trans women.)

It makes more sense to think of misogyny as the continual policing and punishment of certain women for their perceived failures to stay subordinate to men. Rather than trying to eliminate all women, misogynist violence can ironically be quite selective as a way of symbolically threatening all women. Misogyny's discretion is a warning to everyone else: you will be next if you don't fall in line. By blaming its targets—women declared to transgress the boundaries of proper femininity or subservience—misogyny naturalizes and justifies women's broader subordination as a class to men. Manne argues that trans misogyny fits this definition perfectly and reminds us that misogyny is not universal in its expression.

"Violence is a form of entitlement," clarifies the social critic Jacqueline Rose, who also sees the targeting of trans women as a key example of how violence against women operates. "It relies for its persistence on a refusal to acknowledge that it is even there." At the same time, misogynist violence is so vicious and unaccountable because it depends on a lie of superior strength. To dominate or dispose of a trans woman is one way to literalize the wish of domination that is promised but impossible for men to live up to. "No man comfortably possesses masculinity," Rose explains. "Prowess is a lie, as every inch of mortal flesh bears witness. But like all lies, in order to be believed, it has to be endlessly repeated."[21]

These feminist analyses are much sharper than those underlying the criminalization of violence against trans women. Nevertheless, the psychological description still begs bigger questions about the causes and concrete ends that violence against trans women serves. The psychological frame can only answer *why* trans women specifically are subject to so much violence on a surface level. Why do some men fixate so intensely on trans women? Why do they desire trans women in the first place if they sometimes go on to assault, abuse, or even kill them? And why does the subordination of women in general require punishing trans women specifically? The psychological analysis appeals to a vague notion that woman-hating is ubiquitous human behavior, or the result of an overwhelmingly patriarchal culture; but even still, it has not answered questions of causality. Violence against trans women might be understood as a byproduct of widespread trans misogyny as a cultural norm, but this doesn't explain why trans misogyny became so widespread in the first place, where it came from, or how it could be effectively challenged, since neither the law nor psychology have stumbled upon an effective remedy. Yet again, trans women's destiny remains violence, even if the description of how violence transpires interpersonally has improved.

The psychological explanation of trans misogyny doesn't paint a very rosy picture of men, either. Like the overinflated premise of 1970s radical feminism that violence inheres to men, it can't explain why some men act on the widespread trans misogyny structuring the world, but most do not. It can explain trans misogyny or trans panic through an analogy to violence against women, but it can't explain why trans women are often subject to homophobia and gay panic, too. It also can't explain why non-trans women suffer terrible consequences if they are mistaken for being trans, or merely support trans women publicly. Moreover, through the mere addition of *trans* to *violence against women*, or *misogyny*, the role of racism is demoted to an add-on, rather than acknowledged as at its root. In short, psychology, like criminal law, treats trans panic vaguely, almost fearfully, as if there is nothing to be done but denounce violence against trans women and blame men for it. No wonder, then, that for all the calls to action against violence against trans women, few genuine remedies are ever offered. In the wake of the social service model inaugurated by *transgender* in the 1990s, where the self-appointed custodians of trans women refused to accept the words girls on the street used to name themselves, explanations for violence seem to likewise avoid listening to what trans women know about violence, or want to do about it. Such refusal to invest in the people who know the violence best is surely part of the reason it remains a spectacle of pleasure and avoidance for the public, who enjoy consuming it. But if men are not inherently evil and trans women do not intrinsically invite reprisal—which would make the violence unstoppable—then the psychology of that violence had to arise at a certain place and time. Trans panic had to be invented.

For nearly two centuries, everyone but trans women have monopolized the meaning of trans femininity. Fearful of interdependence, many have tried to violently wish trans femininity away. The non-trans woman has become gender critical, willing to dispose of her trans sister to secure her claim on womanhood. The gay man celebrates queens as iconic but separates himself anxiously from faggotry's intimacy with trans femininity, claiming he is only on the side of sexuality, not gender. The straight man acts out in violence to disavow his desire for the girls he watches in porn, the girls he cheats on his wife with, and the girls from whom he buys sex. The state has used trans femininity most of all to generate the pretense it needs to expand its sovereignty as a monopoly on violence. And even queer and trans people, whether as cultural producers, activists, or scholars, have used the symbolic value of trans femininity to guarantee their political authenticity.

But this is only to tell half of the story. The anxious and angry rejection of everyone's interdependence with trans women is an attempt to refuse a social debt accrued, to refuse the power trans femininity holds. The story of interdependence is also the story of trans womanhood and trans femininity, of a tradition that has formed alongside and in response to trans misogyny. *A Short History of Trans Misogyny* tells a story in four acts that valorizes the experience, genius, and desires of trans women and trans femininity in the face of misogyny, racism, poverty, and state violence. Rather than use the distinction between trans women and trans femininity to demean or segregate, this book speaks in multiple tongues to make clear that trans femininity is central to everyone: too powerful, too ubiquitous, and too much in everyone's business to be contained by any word. Trans womanhood as a way of life is not always coincident with trans femininity as an ascribed appearance, an aesthetic and embodied repertoire, or an abstract idea. To denude the American and European colonizing project that has long made use of gender to extend its false universalism, this book adds the phrase *trans-feminized* to describe what happens to groups subjected to trans misogyny though they did not, or still do not, wish to be known as transgender women. In fact, the trans-feminization of populations to dispossess them of Indigenous ways of life, kinship structures, languages, social roles, and political values is one of the central histories of trans misogyny this book examines. Trans misogyny offers a perspective more sophisticated than any identity- or language-driven analysis because it does not presume in advance that trans femininity or trans womanhood are inherently emancipatory, or even shared and stable categories. Black, Brown, and Indigenous trans-feminized people have often rejected the arrival of *trans* as a missionary force from the global North, or have been forced to work within its limiting parameters to survive.

A Short History of Trans Misogyny tells a series of global stories from the early nineteenth century to the present day. By calling them "global," I don't mean that trans misogyny or trans femininity are ubiquitous. On the contrary, the word *global* is meant in a devastating sense, as an index of the saturating reach of both colonial and capitalist projects that have violently homogenized land, cultures, languages, religions, and labor into a single planetary system. The nonredemptively *trans* threads of global histories of colonialism and capital have been scandalously neglected by scholars, cultural critics, and activists in the global North. But why frame the history of trans women and trans femininity through the lens of misogynist violence and trans-feminization? Doesn't that risk reinforcing the link between trans misogyny and being trans feminine? The truth might be quite the opposite. Despite the growing awareness that trans women's hypervisibility—especially for those who are racialized, or who are sex workers and migrants—puts them at risk of some of the highest rates of violence in the world, there are shockingly few tools to answer what remains perhaps the most important question: Why does such potent and extreme trans misogyny characterize nearly the entire world? Why does it transpire in radically different cultural and political contexts? Why is trans misogyny advanced by both ultraconservative, authoritarian movements and left-wing feminists? Why is trans misogyny part of a broader attack on LGBT people in some places, and directed at trans women by gays and lesbians in others? What is the political purpose of trans misogyny? And where did it first emerge?

These are not rhetorical questions. Without a clear definition, history, and understanding of trans misogyny as a concrete form of documentable violence, we risk being left in the zone of vague moral theories. Trans misogyny, like the vague concept of transphobia, becomes some sort of quasi-religious bigotry or hatred that has apparently always existed and waits for convenient moments to erupt.[22] Trans misogyny, in other words, becomes another Euro-American idea projected onto the rest of the world to make it universal. But if it were so, then trans misogyny would be such a deeply irrational kind of hatred that it would be impossible to rid the world of it. And without a clear understanding of what distinguishes *trans* misogyny from broader misogyny, or its connections to homophobia, we risk collapsing the political differences between trans and non-trans women, as well as leaving the door open to trans-exclusionary feminists to characterize trans women as "privileged males" who don't experience misogyny at all.

For that reason alone, painful as it may be to reconstruct such a long and meticulous history, trans misogyny needs to be studied in detail. This book does so by examining the emergence and spread of a specific pattern of sexualized, feminizing violence that began to trans-feminize people living under the designs of colonialism in the nineteenth century. This is not the usual history-of-medicine approach to trans history, where the psychiatric concepts of transvestism or transsexuality are first composed in the halls of science in Berlin, Paris, London, and New York. Nor is it a social movement history. The prototypical target of trans misogyny is not a patient of

Magnus Hirschfeld but a *hijra* in British India, a free Black woman living in the shadow of the transatlantic slave trade in the United States, and a Two-Spirit person facing cultural genocide in the Americas, each of whom was uprooted from a way of life that had no relationship to *trans* but for state violence, colonialism, and the political economy of industrial capitalism. Rather than assuming in advance that modern trans women's history began in the West and then subsequently spread through colonialism around the globe, the flow is not so much reversed as multidirectional. People adopting trans womanhood as a way of life in the nineteenth century—namely, by dressing as women, going by women's names, and practicing sex work—did so not only in New York City, London, and Berlin but in the colonial red-light districts of the British, French, Dutch, German, and American empires.

Trans misogyny formed first as a mode of colonial statecraft that modeled for individuals how to sexualize, dehumanize, and aggress trans-feminized people through panic, beginning with police officers. While trans women of various sorts preexisted the nineteenth century, it is only in its second half that a pattern targeting them for being trans feminine arises. Earlier trans women, like Mary Jones, a sex worker who was arrested in New York City in 1836, were treated as spectacles, not because they lived as women but for the perceived threat of their racial comportment. Jones, a free Black woman, was charged in the court of public opinion with "amalgamation" —taking white men as clients—not for trespassing the line between the sexes. But by the end of the century, as memoirist Jennie June was meeting up with working-class men in New York, she narrated the violence she and other trans-feminized people faced on the street in terms that sound strikingly familiar to the present day. Although the men she went on dates with "liked to flirt with me an hour in the park as if I were a full-fledged mademoiselle," June had to carefully manage the moment of disclosure—something that Jones had not.[23] The reason June had to be careful was not that men would discover she was trans, but that they sought her out *because* she was visibly trans to them. Decades earlier, by contrast, Jones was not visibly trans on the street to her fellow New Yorkers. By June's time, as now, the combination of visibility and desire could turn deadly. The pattern of street violence she describes at the end of the nineteenth century has remained surprisingly stable over time and in its saturation of the globe, with high rates of murder and assault persisting to this day—documented not only in the United States but in countries ranging from Brazil to Greece to Kazakhstan to Malawi.[24] The long duration and stability of violence is a robust and rigorous, if deeply disturbing, piece of evidence for trans misogyny's historicity.

By focusing on the history of trans misogyny, however, this book does not pretend to author a definitive history of trans womanhood. In fact, the takeaway is emphatically the opposite: I do not think a coherent history of trans women is possible, or worth attempting. Clearly there have been people in nearly every recorded human culture who have lived in the roles of women, or in between specific understandings of manhood and womanhood, despite not having inherited that role at birth or through anatomy.[25] However, to deduce that trans women as we know them today have "always existed" would be foolish for several reasons. First, there is no meaningful way to land on a definition of trans femininity that could apply to all places and times, much like there is no way to agree on a single definition of womanhood. It has largely been people from the global North who have romanticized non-Western, Indigenous, and ancient societies into a self-serving and ethnocentric definition of trans femininity that mirrors their own.[26] How do the socially high-status *'aqi* of the Chumash people of present-day California, responsible for handling burial practices; the stigmatized *renyao* (translatable as "human ghost" or "monster") in China and Taiwan; and the *fa'afafine* of the Samoan diaspora, for example, unify into something shared with trans women in the US, Europe, or Australia?[27] More pointedly, a staggering array of non-Western cultures have been irreparably marked by the reductive violence of colonialism, which included the enforcement of a male/female sex binary in which trans life acquired its present association with boundary-crossing.[28] Trans-feminization as a concept responds to this problem, emphasizing that labeling many kinds of people "trans women" is continuous with that colonial project. Even for groups with documented histories spanning hundreds or thousands of years, like hijras in South Asia, the legacy of colonialism has so transformed their social and political standing that they are now caught by LGBT politics on one side and by religious nationalism on the other.[29]

By Euro-American standards, trans womanhood today is construed as an individual identity, a kind of personal property held deep within the self that creates conflict with families of origin, public norms, and social institutions. In many other contemporary cultures, and in many time periods prior to the present, however, a trans-feminine way of life has not necessarily required leaving kinship structures behind or adopting an identity positioned against social norms, or even crossing boundaries at all.

While no one but the most delirious imperialist can innocently survey the globe to put a single stamp on trans womanhood or trans femininity, it is possible to narrate the global creation of trans misogyny through colonial and class-based arrangements of sex, gender, and sexuality. Instead of presuming trans femininity's coherence in advance and then using history to certify it, this book examines where and when trans femininity became a fault line in broader histories, including the repressive practices of colonial government, the regulation of sex work, the policing of urban space, and the line between the formal and informal economy. In this way, the method of this book is deceptively simple: it uses the history of trans misogyny to understand where trans-feminized people were lit up by the clutches of violence and how they responded to its aggressions. In doing so, we learn what makes trans misogyny unique *and* get a glimpse at how wildly diverse people around the world have come to find themselves implicated in trans femininity and trans womanhood, whether or not they wanted to be.

For these reasons, I maintain a difference between *trans femininity* and *trans womanhood* or *trans women*. The first is meant to signal a broad classification by outside observers, including aesthetic criteria and the history of ideas attached to people who have been trans-feminized. Trans *womanhood* and *women*, on the other hand, name people who saw themselves as intentionally belonging to a shared category—in other words, who tried to live in the world recognized as women, whatever that category meant to them contextually. Everyone in this book may have been *trans-feminized*, and all may have been brought into the orbit of *trans femininity*, but only some considered themselves to be *trans women* in response. These careful, empirical distinctions remind that trans misogyny has had the effect of pulling huge swaths of people into relation with one another, like Black trans women in New York City and *kathoeys* in Bangkok, who but for the accidents of history may never have seen each other as having anything in common. It does not weaken the category of trans femininity, or the political project of trans feminism, to examine trans women alongside hijras, street queens, transvestites, and Two-Spirit people, even if few to none of the latter would identify as trans women. On the contrary, it reveals just how narrow the Western definition of *woman* has been, since many groups of people reject it as a colonial limitation, even when it arrives in a trans idiom.

Some of the fault lines this book explores remain sources of major friction to this day. Is trans femininity best understood in relation to womanhood, or does its history suggest that gay men's culture is its better reference? Much would seem to be at stake in the answer, for if trans women are *women*, period, as the adage goes today, why does so much of their history involve gay men? From late-nineteenth-century sexology's concept of "the invert" to present-day fights over whether trans women belong in drag, the mixing of gender and sexual frameworks has long produced anxiety directed at trans femininity. Rather than pretend that deciding in one direction or the other is desirable, let alone possible, *A Short History of Trans Misogyny* emphasizes how gender and sexuality, or what is gay and what is trans feminine, have generally been blurred for most people. This book explores what kind of womanhood trans women acquire by doing sex work and considers the street queens of the mid-twentieth century who answered to the word *gay* precisely because their trans femininity had made them the queens of something called "the gay world." Gay men turned to them to reflect on the electrifying promise—or horrifying possibility—of falling down the proverbial rabbit hole from effeminacy into outright femininity. Street queens appear all over the gay male cultural canon because their proximity to gay men represented the threat and freedom of "going all the way."

Trans women and trans femininity, from this book's perspective, aren't so definitively excluded or erased as they are degraded and punished by those who lust after them in anger, fascination, and affection. Though I bracket trans-femininized people from other kinds of trans people—namely, trans men—this book has no separatist impulse. It doesn't argue that trans women or trans femininity must be taken up in isolation to do them justice, or that trans misogyny is the responsibility of any single group, including men. Nor does it subscribe to the simplistic notion that some kinds of people are inherently affected by trans misogyny while others are cleanly exempt from it. *A Short History of Trans Misogyny* stresses that gender categories are intensely social, even if they are arranged in hierarchies. Trans femininity, just like non-trans womanhood or male heterosexuality, doesn't come into the world on an island. Each one of us emerges as individuals to know ourselves only through our entangled relationships to those who are not like us—which is, strictly speaking, everyone. Indeed, the root fear common to trans-misogynist women, gay men, straight men, nonbinary people, or even certain trans women comes from needing the trans femininity of others as a foil for their place in the world.

Gender as a system coerces and maintains radical interdependence, regardless of anyone's identity or politics. Trans misogyny is one particularly harsh reaction to the obligations of that system—obligations guaranteed by state as much as by civil society. The more viciously or evangelically any trans misogynist delivers invectives against the immoral, impolitic, or dangerous trans women in the world, the more they admit that their gender and sexual identities depend on trans femininity in a crucial way for existence.

Understanding this primary interdependence between gender and sexual positions in the hegemonic Western system, this book pairs trans-feminized subjects in each chapter with people whose relationships to them are disavowed in misogyny. By telling stories through their enmeshment, this book refuses to pretend that trans-feminized people are alone, isolated, and suffering because they need rescue. This book refuses to pretend there is only one form that trans womanhood and trans femininity take, or that the Western model of gender identity and bourgeois individualism, with its simplistic understanding of oppression, is all that useful except as a tool of discipline and domination. And though it cannot tabulate every relevant entry in what would be an impossibly long list, this book insists on holding everyone accountable for the degradation of trans femininity. The collective power of trans-feminized people, including trans women, lies in how many others rely on us to secure their claim to personhood.

In other words, the dolls hold all the receipts, and the time has come to call them in.

❧

This book investigates three of trans misogyny's most enduring manifestations: trans panic, the downward mobility of embracing womanhood under wage-labor capitalism, and the betrayal of trans femininity in the post-Stonewall gay movement. Each chapter asks why trans women and trans femininity have been intensely mistreated by straight men, non-trans women, and gays and lesbians, rather than assuming the answer is self-evident; each, in turn, details how that mistreatment has formed a stable pattern for two centuries.

Chapter 1, "The Global Trans Panic," narrates the emergence of a recognizable form of state violence called trans panic and tracks its stability from the nineteenth century to the 2020 pardon of an American soldier stationed in the Philippines for murdering a trans woman. Pairing trans women with the straight men who desire them, buy sex from them, and frequently commit violence against them with state-sanctioned impunity, the chapter takes the trans panic defense used today and works backward to its antecedents. It explores the example of a British colonial campaign against trans-feminized hijras in India, whose planned eradication established the signature killability that began to attach to trans femininity over the course of the century.

The global trans panic is the most spectacular and injurious lens through which trans femininity has come into the purview of the modern world. Chapters 1 and 2 show that the nineteenth-century state invented this tactic. Entire populations, including hijras, Two-Spirit peoples, and enslaved Africans found their ways of life ripped from them by colonialism and the slave trade, replaced with accusations of corrupt sexuality and improper gender. By sexualizing, misgendering, and even ungendering some of them as exceptions to the so-called natural history of civilization, the state justified immense violence to consolidate its sovereignty, its claims to stolen land, and its function as guarantor of private property. Hijras were put on police registries, beaten in the street, and had their property stolen, disrupting their ascetic way of life. Two-Spirit peoples were abducted from their kinship networks in childhood, placed in residential schools, and systematically abused out of their language, bodies, and spirit. Black trans women found their entire lives criminalized in the aftermath of emancipation, facing police brutality on the street, cycles of incarceration, and satirical contempt from the public. The global trans panic of the nineteenth century helped justify the occupations, governments, and trafficking that fueled colonialism, transatlantic slavery, and the growing hegemony of industrial capitalism. These massive upheavals, displacements, genocidal campaigns, and regimes of policing set the terms for how Black, Brown, and Indigenous trans-feminized people would experience their lives thereafter. By casting trans femininity as a spectacle of excess and moral corruption, the state hedged its monopoly on legitimate violence. Moral panics targeting trans femininity continue to be a popular form of statecraft to this day, especially in the rubble of empire.

Chapter 2, "Sex and the Antebellum City," asks why trans womanhood is so strongly associated with sex work. The answer comes in the remarkable life of Mary Jones. During her trial for grand larceny Jones was sensationalized in the press, but this also testified to the social and economic mobility she had leveraged out of Black gender through sex work. In an era during which wage labor was only beginning to replace legal slavery, Jones worked the contradictions between mobility and incarceration ensnaring free Black people to live as a woman. Her way of life is a portal to the historical relationship between the service economy and racialized trans femininity. The chapter details some of the ways of life and labor that arose in the world birthed by the global trans panic. Dispossessed of kinship ties and land, trans-feminized people were pushed into growing cities by their downward mobility, and they monetized trans femininity in nightlife and sex work. Trans women made the simultaneous mobility of industrializing cities and their regimes of criminalization pay on the unique value of being "public women." And, around the world, people lined up to pay them, from sporting men in antebellum New York to cabaret audiences in Weimar Germany to American soldiers stationed in the Philippines. Trans femininity tied itself to the political economy of the street—the place to which anyone barred from the formal economy flocked.

The third chapter, "Queens of the Gay World," sticks with the street in a love letter to its queens. Fixtures of the gay underworld, street queens fascinated gay men and were memorialized in literature and on screen, from Miss Destiny in John Rechy's *City of Night* (1963), to Crystal LaBeija in *The Queen* (1968), to Venus Xtravaganza in *Paris Is Burning* (1990). The uncertain line between an effeminate gay man and a trans woman wasn't so ironclad in the 1950s and '60s, when it functioned as a class distinction. Street queens, unlike the glamorous and enviable drag performers of the stage, were considered trashy for trying to live as real women, in plain sight. In the contest over their place in gay life, their promise to reign as divine queens and deliver gay people to an abundant world free from stigma and poverty spilled into the aftermath of the Stonewall rebellion in 1969. Gay and lesbian political movements ultimately betrayed trans femininity in the early 1970s to secure their respectability as men and women. This chapter tells an unconventional story of two legends of LGBT history by pairing Sylvia Rivera and Marsha P. Johnson with the fictional Miss Destiny in Rechy's novel—for all three were street queens, a fact often overlooked in their legacy.

The 1970s were also the moment that Western feminism had a falling out with trans women. At the West Coast Lesbian Conference in Los Angeles in 1973, the folk singer Beth Elliot, one of the conference organizers, got onstage to perform. But before she could begin, two other women took away the microphone. One declared, "He is a transsexual and a rapist!" and demanded she not be allowed to play. A few audience members tried to physically attack Elliot, but she was protected by other performers. Eventually, the organizers took a poll of the crowd, who strongly wanted her to go on. Elliot played.

The next morning the conference keynote speaker, a well-known feminist writer named Robin Morgan, gave a speech she had furiously revised the night before, denouncing women like Elliot. Morgan's rhetoric announced many of the hallmarks of feminist trans misogyny:

> Thirty-two years of suffering in an androcentric society, and of surviving, have earned me the name "woman" ... One walk down the street by a male transvestite, five minutes of his being hassled (which he may enjoy), and then he dares, he dares, to think he understands our pain? No, in our mother's names and in our own, we must not call him sister. We know what's at work when whites wear blackface; the same thing is at work when men wear drag.

Morgan, who was white, followed the blackface metaphor by calling women like Elliot rapists, at least in "mentality."[30] Her keynote speech remains one of the most cited events through which trans-exclusionary feminism, particularly in a lesbian register, came into existence.

This book gives little space to trans-exclusionary feminism because it has had far less impact on trans women and trans-feminized people than colonialism, the policing of public space, the criminalization of sex work, and the betrayal of street queens. The emergence of trans-exclusionary radical feminism in the 1970s, with its own version of trans panic, is only one of many trans-misogynist echoes in recent history. TERFs, as they are now often called, didn't invent trans misogyny, nor did they put a particularly novel spin on it. Morgan's speech may have presented an aggrieved and victimized woman as the righteous subject of feminism, but her portrayal of trans femininity as violent and depraved could have been lifted from the British denunciation of hijras in the 1870s, or from

Nazi propaganda about transvestites in the 1930s. It's also untrue that American feminists, even lesbian feminists, were solidly anti-trans in the 1970s. Recent work by historians has cast doubt on how popular TERF beliefs ever were outside of a few loud agitators—as Elliot's overwhelming support at the conference testified.[31] If anything, TERFS, whether in the 1970s or in their contemporary "gender-critical" guise, are better understood as conventional boosters of statist and racist political institutions. As scholar Kyla Schuller explains in *The Trouble with White Women*, anti-trans feminism places itself in a nineteenth-century tradition of white feminist politics in the US and the UK, where white women claim an ordained role in governing others justified through a simplistic sense of gender separatism. "Trans-exclusionist feminists adhere to a single-axis model of power in which sexism is the basic, underlying, most fundamental social inequality. Capitalism and colonialism, and the racism that fuels their engines, lay relatively inert. Instead, maleness or femaleness alone pins one's place in the social hierarchy and determines individual behavior," writes Schuller. "As a result, TERFs argued that liberation can only take place if men are absent. Theirs is a white feminist separatism."[32]

It's difficult to imagine a scarcity mindset more fearful and vengeful than anti-trans feminism, which solipsistically blames all men for all violence but only demands the punishment of trans women, ignoring racism, colonialism, and capitalism. Anti-trans feminism in the UK and US envisions a ruling class of white women who would police everyone else because they have declared them inferior and dangerous. But trans-exclusionary feminism has frankly played a minor role in trans misogyny until quite recently, when it has surged to new mainstream legitimacy. Taking a historical point of view, debunking anti-trans feminism offers little to the cause of building genuine trans-feminist movements. TERFs, like the right-wing evangelicals or white supremacists who agree with them politically, are not the lynchpin to trans misogyny; rather, they are at best one of its latest symptoms.

This book's conclusion, "Mujerísima and Post-scarcity Feminism," poses a bold new trans feminism for the twenty-first century and critiques the flaccid trans misogyny of the present in both anti-trans feminism and queer and trans movements. Dissatisfied with the impotence of trans-inclusive feminism, which has proven unable to outmaneuver the trans misogyny of gender-critical and far-right anti-trans political movements, the book turns to trans feminisms in Latin America for a different lesson. The word *mujerísima* contends that trans women are not just women but *the most woman*, or *super-feminine*. Each chapter of *A Short History of Trans Misogyny* details one way trans women have been targeted for that exceptional femininity. Acknowledging that mainstream liberal and Western feminism has also repudiated femininity in a quest to equal men, the book ends with a feminism led by the loudest and most exalted femininity, refusing all concessions. This trans feminism is one that Spanish- and Portuguese-speaking *travestis* in Latin America sometimes champion to challenge the international order of state power and shallow human rights being codified as the progressive consensus of *trans*. A trans feminism characterized by mujerísima may be strong enough to break with the history of trans misogyny and the limitations of confining feminism to the proper definition of "women." Instead of perpetuating the myth that trans-feminized people in the global South need leadership or rescuing by trans people from the global North, the conclusion asks everyone to listen to the wisdom and tenacity of travestis.

Spanning nearly two centuries of global history, the basic pattern of trans misogyny is much older than TERFs, or right-wing Christians, and extremely consistent. Trans misogyny is not a mere psychological and irrational hatred of trans women. In fact, trans misogyny as a concept helps explain how individuals, or interpersonal violence, can act on behalf of the state or other abstract political movements. At the interpersonal scale, however, trans misogyny testifies to the uncomfortable thickness of social bonds across hierarchies of gender, class, and race. When a straight man lashes out after dating or having sex with a trans woman, he is often afraid of the implication that his sexuality is joined to hers. When a gay man anxiously keeps trans women out of his activism or social circles, he is often fearful of their common stigma as feminine. And when a non-trans feminist claims she is erased by trans women's access to a bathroom, she is often afraid that their shared vulnerability as feminized people will be magnified intolerably by trans women's presence. In each case, trans misogyny displays a fear of interdependence and a refusal of solidarity. It is felt as a fear of proximity. Trans femininity is too sociable, too connected to everyone—too exuberant about stigmatized femininity—and many people fear the excess of trans femininity and sexuality getting too close. But sociability can never be confined or blamed on one person in a relationship; it's impersonal, and it sticks to everyone.

The defensive fear and projection built into trans misogyny, whether genuine or performed, is an attempt to wish away what it nonetheless recognizes: that trans femininity is an integral part of the social fabric. There will be no emancipation for anyone until we embrace trans femininity's centrality and value.

What follows is a short history of the trans misogyny that has constructed the shared world.

1

The Global Trans Panic

Long before it was a legal defense, in the nineteenth century, the global trans panic began. Although it had no single beginning or architect, traces of its emergence are archived in the Northwestern Provinces of colonial India. Like all the subdivisions of British India, the NWP was more a wishful declaration than proof of colonial power. For over a century, the British East India Company's military and economic power crept across the subcontinent, making India a bloated corporate ploy. As a result, British sovereignty was weak. To maintain power, British officials relied enormously on Indian elites. Hundreds of princely states were allowed to retain their customary authority, and the British cultivated a growing middle class of Indian functionaries educated in English. Still, the gap between lines on a map drawn in London and reality on the ground was enormous. In 1857, the Indian Rebellion rocked the region; Indian soldiers recruited to maintain colonial order mutinied, and the British effectively lost most of the North. Only after months of vicious fighting did the British manage to regain military control. Fearful that their position remained insecure, British India was formalized as a colony under the Crown, dissolving East India Company rule. The Northwestern Provinces, one of the most staunchly anticolonial regions during the rebellion, were an administrative result of the anxious consolidation. British officials feared they might lose the NWP again, especially because they didn't know much about who lived within its borders. As such, administrators became convinced they needed to pacify Indian society to avoid future rebellion.[1]

It was in this context that the British trans panic in India took root, but its initial spark had come in 1852. That year, a *hijra* named Bhoorah was murdered, and her lover, Ali Buksh, was charged with the crime. Colonial officials weren't at first certain what a hijra was. The occasional European traveler had written about them, like Baltazard Solvyns in his 1810 description of a "Hidgra," whom he classified as "an hermaphrodite." Solvyns's entry in a book of Indian ethnological types railed against people he described as a "vile class of beings" "whose whole life is an outrage to morality and common decency." What was their crime? Living as women having been born male. "Some Hindoos," wrote Solvyns, "believe that they are really born in this state; but it is certain that it is inflicted on them in their earliest infancy by their parents." He also remarked on their visible presence in public and at important moments in family life, like the birth of the child. In Solvyns's estimation, hijras "infest as vagabonds the streets and bazars."[2]

In truth, hijra history is extremely long, complex, and difficult to reconstruct. But in the mid-nineteenth century, hijras were found throughout the subcontinent. They were known for performing in public, mostly by dancing and singing. And they demanded *badhai*, gifts of money to which they were spiritually entitled at the birth of a child, or a marriage. The role of hijras in blessing and supporting the reproduction of the household was tied to their unique and sacred infertility. Hijras may have been born male, but in early childhood they were usually initiated into a discipleship through which they lived as girls. Although they were popularly associated with castration, not all hijras in the 1850s underwent surgery. It was their asceticism that distinguished them: hijras were one of many types of ascetics throughout the subcontinent who lived, at times, at a great distance from British notions of gender, family, and religion.[3]

To understand what happened in the wake of Bhoorah's murder, it's important to say that hijras were not then—and are not today—transgender. Even though the story of the global trans panic weaves through their experience, it doesn't mean they should be interpreted as trans women. Hijras, for one thing, are arguably much older than the Western concept of gender through which trans emerged as boundary cross-ing. They are also much older than the modern concepts with which trans people in Europe and the United States would be identified later in the nineteenth century. In contemporary India, anthropologist Vaibhav Saria explains, hijras are caught in complex political struggles between Hindu nationalists and postcolonial pluralists, not always lining up with Indian transgender activism.[4] Although hijra ways of life had been strongly influenced by centuries of Mughal Islamic rule, they still moved relatively independently of British concepts of sex and gender before English colonialism threatened their way of life. The global trans panic was a pivotal period in which hijras were pulled into the orbit of the Western gender system. The next chapter will explore the political economy of sex work that accounts for how other populations like hijras around the world became linked during this period; this chapter begins that story by showing that the targeting of groups like hijras involved a specific pattern of state-sponsored violence that I term a trans panic. In short, this chapter argues that the vio-lence of a trans panic made hijras trans feminine in the eyes of the British. Over time, colonial trans-femininization began to alter hijras' self-perceptions, but that process trailed the immediate disruption of their way of life. I use the term *trans-feminization* to describe this process in a nonredemptive, even devastating sense. One of the features of trans panic—and trans misogyny more broadly—is that it marks populations as trans feminine, or trans-feminizes them, in spite of however they understand themselves.

There is little reason to trust the colonial court's account of Bhoorah's death, but it does tie the global trans panic to a murder. At the trial of Ali Buksh, the court decided he had killed Bhoorah out of jealousy after she left him for another man. Witnesses described the pair as having quarreled in the street on the night of her death. But the court also declared that Bhoorah had been a prostitute. The judge used his verdict to pronounce a moral sermon alerting colonial officials to what he considered an immoral hijra underground about which something had to be done. Judge Unwin's statement, as historian Jessica Hinchy explains, treated Bhoorah's death as the tip of the iceberg of a mysterious "eunuch problem." (British officials rarely used the term *hijra*.)

"The sickening details of this case," wrote Unwin, "involve the disgusting exposure of an abominable trade in prostitution carried on by eunuchs dressed as women, whom they resemble also in shape, with vested rights to contributions at weddings, &c. in certain villages allotted to one or more of them under a sort of acknowledged internal government." "They have in fact a King," warned the judge, "according to some residents in Delhi, others say at Furruckabad."[5]

Judge Unwin was wrong about most of what he claimed. Hijras were not predominately sex workers, nor did they have a king. But it was a compelling story, one that incited a trans panic in the colonial bureaucracy. The immorality of hijras who trespassed the boundary between men and women by British standards became in Unwin's hands a concrete threat to be put down. The court sexualized hijra gender transgression by calling it prostitution, making it concrete in an era when a central British alibi for empire was ending the global sex trade.[6] Sexual immorality was, crucially, interpreted as a political threat to colonial rule. As Hinchy explains, "What the British didn't know drove the hijra panic."[7] Precisely because the British did not understand what it meant to be a hijra, they invented a story they could understand and that served imperial interests. The idea that hijras were male prostitutes with a secret government became the pretext for a statewide campaign to secure moral order by exterminating them.

In 1865 the NWP adopted an official policy to "reduce" the number of hijras through measures that would "gradually lead to their extinction."[8] Since there was no hijra king to depose, the state aimed to disrupt their livelihoods by breaking up their discipleship system and criminalizing their presence in public. In 1871 the colonial government passed the Criminal Tribes Act (CTA), the second half of which set out procedures targeting hijras. Castration was already illegal, which, along with the allegation of prostitution, made hijras easy targets for the police. But the CTA specifically mandated that hijras submit to a police registry. Not only did the police collect intelligence and personal information, making it easier to identify and subject hijras to surveillance, the registry also took an inventory of their property. The CTA outlawed property inheritance in hijra households, impoverishing them by disrupting their lineages. The law also restricted hijras from traveling outside their local districts, which they often did to attend marriages and births. Combined with the criminalization of dancing in public and wearing women's clothing, their entire way of life was now illegal.[9]

In the nineteenth century, the British empire generally opted for repressive taxation or forced labor over genocide in trying to put down Indigenous populations outside of white settler colonies like Canada and Australia. The Criminal Tribes Act's first half reflected that preference. Using an old North Indian concept of *thags* (thugs), the law allowed the state to label any population standing in its way a criminal gang. The CTA was intended to pacify these so-called criminal tribes to avoid future rebellion. Preventing them from roaming the countryside, this crackdown on their mobility would force them into work that kept them closer to their homes, disconnected from one another and less of a threat to colonial sovereignty. What made hijras different, requiring a separate section under the law, was that the British felt they could never be reformed. Hard labor would not make them into men; rather, hijras were so feminine they were regarded as ungovernable. Cloaked in the homophobia, misogyny, and racism of British attitudes toward "sodomy," sex work, and disease, colonial officials treated hijras as a kind of "doomed race" destined to die out.[10]

Although the British labeled them prostitutes, hijras were treated differently from Indian sex workers, who were also registered by the police and often imprisoned on public health grounds—a difference that starts to explain what constitutes trans panic. Unlike women sex workers, colonial observers considered hijras to be engaged in "professional sodomy," adding a loaded moral outrage to the accusation of sex work.[11] But the British concept of sodomy was also famously vague. The Christian emphasis on not describing the immoral sexual act made criminal conviction for sodomy almost impossible. Since sex left behind no obvious evidence, what could prove sodomy if witnesses would not disclose what they had seen? At the end of the century, the crime of sodomy would be memorialized as "the love that dare not speak its name" at Oscar Wilde's trial. But decades earlier, cross-dressing was used as its practical proof. In 1870, the English press erupted when two "men" in women's clothing were arrested in London and charged as sodomites. They hadn't been caught having sex; they were arrested simply because of the clothes they were wearing. The Boulton and Park case helped cement the link between wearing women's clothes and sodomy. In India, colonial officials adopted the same approach, arguing that the women's clothes hijras wore seduced men into sodomy. The threat of hijras dressed as women in public was treated as so morally severe—and politically dangerous to the colonial state—that nothing less than the total eradication of all hijras could squash it.[12]

As Hinchy's invaluable research on the hijra panic shows, the CTA was not very successful. Although many hijras were registered in some districts in the NWP, others registered very few. Most hijras were able to outwit the police in everyday life because there were too few officers to consistently enforce the law. Some petitioned the colonial government protesting their registration, and a few were even "deregistered." The law manifestly failed in its extreme goal of exterminating the population, and its implementation withered by the end of the century. But the assault on the hijra way of life did have lasting consequences. For one, the law led to an escalation in police violence wherever it was applied. In one NWP district, a police officer reported that he would seek out hijras in public, cut their hair, strip them of their clothes and jewelry, and then force them into men's clothing. The loss of income from singing, dancing, and badhai likewise proved lasting.[13] This had less to do with the CTA, which was not applied much beyond the NWP, and more to do with the staggering impoverishment of the Indian population under British rule. Hijras were one of many social groups of Indians whose public lives were criminalized as "nuisances," but the economic disruption of their way of life under colonialism was devastating. When it came to the division of public and private labor, British society was organized around a strict separate-spheres ideology. Women were ideally consigned to the home, while labor and public life were intended for men—a division that hijras transgressed simply by going about their daily lives.

Although hijras survived the British trans panic that sought to eradicate them, they were forever changed by the criminalization of that transgression and its disruption of their way life, including their means of making money. For one thing, today hijras often are sex workers. In a present-day ethnography in the Indian province of Odisha, Vaibhav Saria explains that the local hijra population experiences poverty as a structural consequence of their ascetic role in the community having merged symbolically with low pay.[14] Although the intervening history is too complex to reduce to any one cause, the British trans panic in the colonial era seems to have played a lasting role in sexualizing hijras and actually pushing them toward sex work by criminalizing their previous way of life. Thus, through the policing and economic disruption brought about by trans panic, what began as an accusation and a British fiction became the condition of many hijras.

The colonial assault on hijras shows that trans panic first emerged and worked without a distinctive psychology. The British misgendered hijras as a population by sexualizing them as male sodomites and sex workers, ignoring the ascetic role they played in their communities. The conflation of femininity with sodomy was rooted in their clothing and presence in public, both of which flouted British norms and could therefore be read as a threat to imperial sovereignty. The colonial state appointed itself the political right to exterminate hijras to satisfy panicked British moral order. As we have seen, doing so meant ending the hijra way of life, but it also empowered men—namely, police officers—to look for and attack hijras in the street. Their sexualized femininity thus became the target for violent punishment in a way that would recur countless times around the world in a similar pattern. It was in this widespread panic and trans-feminization by the state that individual men learned to experience and wield trans panic, too. Psychology followed the example of the state.

The pattern is shockingly consistent. In the 1870s, halfway around the world in the United States, federal agents began entering Indigenous communities confined on reservations to enforce laws banning religious and cultural practices that the settler state considered threats to its sovereignty. Joe Medicine Crow, an elder in the Crow nation, remembered the campaign one federal agent named Briskow waged against the *badés* in his community during the 1890s. *Badé* (sometimes spelled *baté*) is a Crow word for a respected social role that today might fall under the pan-Indigenous category Two-Spirit. "The agent incarcerated the badés," Joe Medicine Crow told an anthropologist, "cut off their hair, made them wear men's clothing. He forced them to do manual labor," including planting trees that still stand on the reservation—towering memorials to gendered violence. "The people were so upset" with the agent's violence against the badés "that Chief Pretty Eagle came into Crow Agency and told Briskow to leave the reservation." "It was a tragedy," Joes Medicine Crow recalled, "trying to change them."[15]

The striking similarity between the actions of the police officer in the NWP and the federal agent on the Crow Reservation is evidence that the trans panic of the nineteenth century was global in scope. This doesn't mean it was coordinated but rather that colonial states were similarly incentivized to target populations through trans panics as a way of securing sovereignty. Despite the overwhelming differences between colonial India and the settler US, men acting as agents of the state went after people whose femininity was deemed a threat to public order in a consistent manner, violently cutting their hair, removing their clothing and adornments, and demanding they behave like men. Two-Spirit people across the Americas endured these violent assaults on their ways of life as part of a centuries-long project of genocide—or gendercide—as did other countless other populations trans-femininized as "sodomites" by colonial expansion around the globe—from the *babaylan* persecuted by Catholic missionaries in the Spanish colonial Philippines to the *mahu* targeted by Christian missionaries attached to the white planter class in pre-annexation Hawai'i.[16] Colonial states used trans panic as a pretense to secure political and economic power. What was trans about the panic was not that the people being targeted themselves were inherently trans women, but that they were trans-feminized by the conflation of male femininity with immoral sodomy and sex work.

The fact that the state's enforcers were policemen in each case is also important. After all, the global trans panic was not only about the general violence waged against populations now trans-feminized by the state; the panic also inaugurated the killability of trans women on an interpersonal scale. A new relationship between men and trans femininity was taking shape, leading to a world in which trans panic would eventually become the legal defense it remains today.

In 1895, Jennie June decided to spend the summer living in New York City's Stuyvesant Square. The large park on the East side of Manhattan was built around two ornate fountains and flanked by St. George's Church. In the 1890s it was also the heart of a well-known vice district in the city's notorious public-sex economy.[17] June called herself an "androgyne," her fin-de-siècle word for someone raised male who was female in heart and soul. Because she was well educated and wealthy, June read the European medical texts of the day, largely imported from Germany. Sexologists regarded people like her as mixed in sex, with biological attributes both male and female, though their personalities tended to put them at odds with their anatomy. Dressed as a woman, June was determined to live as one whenever she could. She devoted her summer to Stuyvesant Square because she knew it would be a good place to meet working-class men—her type. After a month of promenading and sitting in the park, "I had been introduced to several score young bloods," June wrote in her memoir. "The majority liked to flirt with me an hour in the park as if I were a full-fledged mademoiselle."[18]

One of those long sunny days, June met a man with bright red hair. "He looked to be twenty, was rather shabbily clad, but clean. It was not his features," she recalled, "but his powerful and well proportioned figure, that attracted me." They started flirting. In her memoir *The Female-Impersonators*, June gave him the over-the-top name Hercules. He must have resembled that ideal: youthful, working class, and ruggedly masculine. But those same attributes made him potentially dangerous. "In order to ascertain the trustworthiness, good-heartedness, and liberalmindedness of the Hercules," she wrote, "I first drew him out craftily by a long series of questions." After all, "I expected to put myself in the power of Hercules." If she was going to do *that*, she need to know what kind of man he was.[19]

More than a century before Sam Feder's documentary of the same name, June explained to her readers the problem of "disclosure": telling a partner that you're trans.[20]

After talking a while, June decided Hercules was trustworthy, so she told him she was an androgyne. But her disclosure wasn't exactly a revelation. Hercules already knew. In fact, June also knew that he knew. That was the entire point of their interaction. "From my dress and mannerisms," she explained, "any city-bred youth would have already judged my sexual status. Hercules told me he had, but had feared saying something offensive." By 1895, according to June, working-class men in New York knew what trans femininity looked like, and some of them actively desired girls like her precisely because they were trans. Trans femininity was not only publicly visible in certain neighborhoods; it was seen as different from generic womanhood. It was this street visibility, not invisibility, that created the danger that disclosure tried to manage. By letting Hercules flirt with her first based on her appearance, and then disclosing that she was an androgyne—which he already knew—June could gauge his reaction in stages and flee at the first sign of trouble. And she had good reason to be careful. "I was always ultra-wary of falling into a trap," she wrote. "Androgynes are murdered every few months in New York merely because of intense hatred of effeminacy instilled by education in the breasts of full-fledged males." At the end of *The Female Impersonators*, June included an appendix of newspaper reprints describing several murders of people like her.[21]

In truth, the androgynes whose murder tales she collected were not quite the same as her—and as a middle-class, politically driven author, June was zealous in flattening the difference. They were effeminate "fairies," per the lingo of the era, but they were not fairies who dressed in women's clothes or, like June, considered themselves to be real women. Yet, even so, the difference isn't especially meaningful in historical context. In this era, especially in the working-class world, what is now conventionally separated out in American culture as "gender" and "sexual orientation" were a single category. Seemingly, men killed fairies and trans women for largely the same reasons: their sexualized femininity.

The live wire between desire and violence was hard to defuse, even with disclosure. After flirting for a while, June and Hercules went for a walk toward the East River. As they left the neighborhood, the buildings became increasingly industrial. "As soon as we arrived in an unlighted stone-yard and there was not another soul within hearing," the date turned violent. Hercules revealed himself to be nothing more than "a dyed-in-the-wool criminal—a fiend who would never give a second thought to having just committed murder." He demanded her wallet, and she handed it over. Then he told her to undress, claiming he wanted to see if she had any more money hidden on her.[22]

June tried to protest. "While we argued, I undressed meekly and in unspeakable terror. I realized I might be experiencing the last five minutes of life."[23]

The man—her Hercules—who had started out charming her in the park, now spat insult after accusation at her. "You bastard! You cannibal! Your nature's so disgustin' that every rightminded man would agree your face oughter be used as a butcher's chopping block! And it's me own great joy ter do the job!"[24]

Hercules started hitting June. At some point, she passed out and he left her, presumably for dead. But she survived. "Providence overruled," she put it in her memoir. "As in a number of subsequently similar assaults when I was snatched from the very jaws of death." But something about the experience felt intractable, bigger than bad luck with one bad apple. "I reflected on my lot: To go through my life as a cordially hated bisexual. That was my cross, and I repeated it over and over again."[25]

June's Victorian writing was exceptionally dramatic, but for a reason: she had a political purpose to telling the story of her date with Hercules. *The Female Impersonators*, a sequel to her first memoir, *Autobiography of an Androgyne*, was meant to elicit sympathy in its reader. The highly stylized depiction of "Hercules," including the condescending rendition of his Irish accent and the perfect plot points to their date gone wrong, are hard to take literally. And considering that June was a wealthy woman slumming in Stuyvesant Square, her credibility is undermined by not hailing from the working-class sexual underworld she was dramatizing for a bourgeois readership. Still, precisely because she had the resources to put pen to paper, it's remarkable to encounter a first-person account of trans panic and street violence from 1895 that sounds a lot like how trans women today might describe violence from the men they date. June suggests that by the end of the nineteenth century, trans panic and its characteristic interpersonal violence were routine on the streets of New York City. But if trans panic was already a feature of life in 1895, why is violence against trans women still so poorly understood 120 years later? If trans women were both desirable and killable in New York in 1895, why isn't June's name recited first at every Trans Day of Remembrance?

For one thing, Jennie June has often been poorly remembered by modern observers as Ralph Werther.

The end of the nineteenth-century period of June's memoir is considered by historians a pivotal moment for the emergence of urban gay subcultures in Western Europe and North America. In his landmark book *Gay New York*, historian George Chauncey found a very different culture than the out-and-proud identity model popularized by the post-Stonewall gay movement. Until well into the twentieth century, sexuality was overwhelmingly class and gender based, and the urban world was structured around men's sexual power. The world was not yet divisible into a binary of hetero- and homo-sexuality. In the era in which June was meeting men in city parks, gay people were overwhelmingly defined by their femininity, especially in working-class neighborhoods. The "fairies," as they were popularly called, were recognizable by their waxed eyebrows, powdered cheeks, bright colors, and effeminate body language or speech. Unlike the idea of "same-sex" or homosexuality, it was their difference from men, their femininity, that advertised their availability. Regular men could have sex with fairies without suffering the loss of their masculinity and being considered queer, because fairies were effeminate—culturally legible replacements for women. As long as men played the active role when having sex with fairies, they weren't regarded as any more unusual than men who paid for sex with women.[26] This cultural norm lasted surprisingly long, well into the 1940s. One man who paid a drag queen for blowjobs explained it to a University of Chicago sociologist in 1933 rather plainly: "A man will do when there is nothing else in the world, *preferably a she man, because he is more womanly or closer to a woman* … It felt good because he was impersonating a woman so it was something like having a woman do me."[27] This was a widespread, rather than a subcultural attitude among straight men.

In the burgeoning cities of Western Europe and the United States, sexuality and gender had no major distinction from one another. And though the idioms varied by location and language, the pattern is unmistakable. New York had its fairies and, later, "pansies" who adopted women's names and went by feminine pronouns, as did Chicago, San Francisco, Los Angeles, Washington, DC, St. Louis, and New Orleans. In London and other English cities, they were called "queans" (with an *a*), while Berlin, Munich, Frankfurt and Cologne had its "inverts" and "third sexers" who called each other *Schwester* (sister) and *Tante* (aunt).[28] In the booming working-class entertainment and public sex districts that accompanied the population explosion of industrial Western cities, female impersonators, cross-dressing performers, campy waitresses, streetwalkers, and other theatrical people were the heart of a gay subculture that attracted curious straight slummers and vice cops alike. Yet for decades, historians applied a post-Stonewall gay rubric to these histories, assuming that femininity was merely a symbol that someone was gay by present-day standards.[29]

Reality was much more complicated. (The example of hijras in British India is a reminder that the conflation of gender and sexuality through the stamp of femininity moved throughout the world via colonialism, rather than being an inherent sign of someone's homosexuality.) Feminine gay people like fairies wouldn't have recognized a contemporary, identity-based model of sexuality or gender to begin with. Yet June wasn't like the typical fairies found throughout Manhattan, even if she understood herself to be one of them. Although fairies acted effeminate, or called each other by girl's names, most didn't wear women's clothing. Many cities had recently passed laws against appearing in public in "masquerade," meaning that dressing in women's clothes was a crime. Still, few fairies considered themselves to be women, even if they didn't consider themselves to be normal men. They were content to be "third sexers," or something in between men and women.[30]

But June did try to move through the world dressed as a woman, rather than a fairy with plucked eyebrows, powdered cheeks, and a red tie. And she was not the only one. In *Gay New York*, Chauncey tells the story of a fairy who went by the name Loop the Loop—after the roller coaster at Coney Island. Like June, she lived full time in women's clothing. Unlike June, however, she had a husband. She was also a sex worker, strolling near Prospect Park in Brooklyn with other fairies. Like many sex workers in New York, Loop the Loop paid off the local cops for protection. In 1906 she was interviewed by a doctor, which preserved a glimpse into what made her unique. Loop the Loop's clients wouldn't have mistaken her for a regular woman sex worker, even though she was dressed as one. In her interview she mentions several obvious tells that would give her away, including the hair on her legs. Why didn't she just shave her legs to increase her likelihood of passing? She explained to the doctor that "most of the boys don't mind at all."[31] In other words, she wasn't trying to be mistaken for a regular woman. As Chauncey puts it, Loop the Loop's "efforts at female impersonation would not have persuaded any of his clients that they were having sex with a woman"—because that is not what her clients wanted.[32] They wanted a woman-like fairy, someone more like a contemporary trans woman, although neither description is quite accurate. But they wanted someone like her, nonetheless. If they had wanted to have sex with a boy, or a fairy who camped it up but was advertising what was still called "male" prostitution, large cities had such brothels in ample supply. Those fairy sex workers wouldn't be wearing women's clothing.[33] Loop the Loop, on the other hand, was always in a dress. And if the desire for trans femininity made her job lucrative, it also came with its own latent danger. If "most of the boys don't mind at all," the ones who did might turn out to be like June's Hercules.

Trans-feminine people like Loop the Loop, however they might have regarded themselves, were united by having few options for work. For decades they had been known not only for sex work but for jobs in nightlife and entertainment where dressing as a woman had a built-in alibi. As early as the 1830s, minstrel shows in New Orleans advertised "female impersona-tion," followed by vaudeville and burlesque troupes that toured the South and had long runs in Northern cities, enjoying a heyday from the 1870s to the 1910s. Many stars of these stages dressed as women only for their acts, much like they donned blackface to stoke anti-Black pleasure in their audiences. But a few were interested in leveraging their jobs as female imper-sonators into a more theatrical way of life offstage.[34] Vice squads and moral reformers in Chicago investigating such clubs kept note of the occasional female impersonator who didn't take off women's clothing at the end of the night.[35] One of them, who lived and worked on the South Side of the city, was known as Nancy Kelly.

Kelly had moved to Chicago from New Orleans in 1924, as part of the Great Migration of African Americans fleeing Jim Crow terror and searching for work in the industrial North. Kelly grew up in a brothel owned by an aunt, meaning that by the time she started working as a female impersonator she was well acquainted with the ins and outs of the South Side's vice economy. By the time she started working in drag, she was following in the footsteps of Black queens who had been fixtures in her neighborhood for decades. She worked local clubs as a dancer, where a single good night could earn as much as forty dollars—compared to the measly twelve dollars a week that she earned at her day job as a dishwasher at the YMCA (where Kelly worked dressed as a man). With that kind of extra income during the Great Depression, Kelly could support her extended family. For that kind of money, she was willing to risk the danger of working and going out in public dressed as a woman. For Kelly, femininity was a matter of economics, not the expression of an inner identity.[36]

Years later, she recounted the story of a nightclub, opened in the 1930s, "called 1410 West Roosevelt Road." It wasn't a gay bar, but the owner "was payin' the girls ten dollars a night to do a show, to build up his crowd, you know." Considering she could dance three "shows" a night, the money was hard to ignore. Kelly found out that her friend Jeanne Lerue, another female impersonator, was dancing there. Lerue offered her a spot in the lineup, but other friends tried to talk her out of it. "They'd say, 'Oooh, no! 1410. Uh-huh, no amount of money!' The boys was so hostile. They'd tear your drags off, tear your wigs off ... They would make nasty remarks, call you all kind of 'Sissy motherfuckers' and everything like that."[37]

Despite the club's reputation, Kelly needed the money, so she dropped by a fellow performer's home to borrow an outfit. "Sister," chided the queen when she learned of her plan, "where in the world do you think you're going?" But Kelly had already made up her mind and stepped out into the evening air in drag. Yet another friend on the street tried to stop her, pleading, "Oh, sister, don't do that. They could *kill* you over there." But Kelly pushed past her, climbing onto a streetcar.

Sitting across from an older woman, Kelly knew right away that she was a spectacle: "All this makeup on and eyelashes, you know, and jewelry, and lipstick and ... Cuban-heeled shoes." A "big drunk dude" on board quickly moved in her direction, crowing at her. "Hey Baby! You sure do look good."

"I say, 'Jesus,'" Kelly remembered. "'Cause now I'm gonna have to rustle with him until I get to Roosevelt Road, you know."

The man crudely pushed his way into sitting down beside her, upping the ante. "What's your problem, *man*?" he said to Kelly with an unmistakable emphasis, before making moaning noises at her.

Petrified, Kelly was saved by the old lady across the aisle, who beckoned her. "Come here honey. Come here. Come here honey, sit over here." Kelly took the offer up with a sigh of relief, settling in beside her. "We women are not even safe anymore," the old lady confided. "That old ..." she said, gesturing to the drunk man, "I would like to curse him but I'm a Christian, you know."[38]

As Kelly remembered it, the whole scene traded in thinly veiled tropes of passing and being clocked, but no matter what was left unsaid, it was obvious what was at stake. Looking trans feminine in public was a huge risk to her safety—it didn't matter if she was only dressed that way for work. "Everybody that was on the streetcar was lookin' at me. I didn't say nothin', I just sit there and crossed my legs." The drunk man knew he could threaten Kelly and there wasn't much she could do about it. Just being on the streetcar in women's clothes was illegal, for one thing. While the old woman's Christian charity may have traded in ignorance that Kelly wasn't the same kind of woman as her, the stares of everyone on the streetcar were proof enough that she was probably using that cover to protect a fellow passenger. Kelly arrived at 1410 unscathed, only to find it was just as bad as everyone had warned. "I saw all these little punks out there in the front," she remembered. "My heart fell." She knew right away she was going to have to do what she had just narrowly avoided: fight back. One young man standing outside boasted as she approached the entrance door. "Oh, here she comes. Here she comes. We're gonna beat your mother-fuckin' ass when you come outa there," he seethed.

"And Jeanne Lerue," the queen who had got Kelly the job in the first place? "She was peepin' through the venetian blinds," remembered Kelly.[39] Surely, she was mortified.

The stories of these working-class fairies don't clarify the difference between homosexuality and trans femininity. While Loop the Loop was more recognizably like a contemporary trans woman, Nancy Kelly was more like a gay man who only got up in drag for pay. According to the logic of trans panic, however, this difference was unimportant. What they had in common was an opportunity for a certain kind of life in the overcrowded, overpoliced working-class neighborhoods of New York City and Chicago. Trans femininity was not an expression of an inner gender identity but rather a mode of public appearance that paid, whether through sex work or dancing in a nightclub. The wide variety of working-class fairies, female impersonators, and full-time women from this period corroborate Jennie June's account of street-based violence. Their common experiences suggest that by the late nineteenth century, trans panic and its characteristic violence were a threat to anyone caught in public visibility, men's desire, and the retaliatory violence that conflated femininity with sexual availability. But if trans panic blurred into homophobia

47

and gay panic, these stories raise a second point: what happened in New York, Chicago, London, or Berlin is not the whole story of trans misogyny, or trans femininity. The trans panic born in the nineteenth century was a phenomenon with a global reach, operating on the scale of colonial state power in British India or the Crow Reservation, and on the interpersonal scale of the street in Western European and North American cities.

To understand how and why violence against trans women emerged, we need to be able to connect these two scales. Panic and trans-feminization produced similar experiences for vastly different kinds of people around the world who had little in common—other than being targets. The men who picked up fairies on the street, or who paid to see female impersonators dance in nightclubs, acted out the same structure of violence when they threatened, assaulted, or robbed them as the colonial state in India or the settler-colonial state in America. This was the same violence wielded by municipal police forces that raided bars and locked people up for cross-dressing. The blending of state violence with interpersonal violence is a signature outcome of the global trans panic, a deadly merger that persists to this day.

In the fall of 2014, US Marine Joseph Scott Pemberton was stationed at Naval Base Subic Bay in the Philippines for military training exercises. He was nineteen years old. Pemberton and many of his fellow Marines were granted "liberty," which gave them permission to venture into Olongapo, a city across the bay. On the night of October 11, Pemberton and three friends made their way to a neighborhood dense with bars, restaurants, and hotels that had for over a century catered to US soldiers—and before them to Spanish colonizers. The four Americans walked into a bar named Ambyanz at around a quarter to eleven. Illuminated by a small symphony of neon lights, Ambyanz was known for sex work, a place where servicemen on liberty could meet young Filipinas. It was hardly out of the ordinary for groups of working women to hold court for the night, socializing with successive clusters of soldiers and occasionally leaving with them for less public locations. In the company of his friends, Pemberton met Jennifer Laude at the bar. A stunning beauty a few years older than him, Laude was flanked by three of her friends. Whatever they talked about, it wasn't an especially long conversation. By eleven o'clock, Pemberton left Ambyanz with Laude and her friend Barbie. The trio walked down the street to a nearby hotel, the Celzone Lodge. The bellboy at the front desk checked them in, and Pemberton haggled a little about the rate before they retreated to their room. That same bellboy later recounted seeing Barbie leave first, on her own. Then, a short time later, Pemberton left, also by himself. The Celzone staff later found Laude dead in the bathroom, slumped over the toilet. She had been strangled to death.[40]

What went on in the hotel room wasn't especially hard to piece together. The bellboy's testimony, together with security camera footage, showed that Pemberton, Barbie, and Laude went into the room together, but that Pemberton and Laude were alone before she died. And when Pemberton returned to base to make curfew, he confessed to a friend that he had killed Laude. But Pemberton claimed a specific justification: he felt he had been deceived by Laude, who was a trans woman. When the three of them had first arrived at the hotel room, Laude and Barbie had given him oral sex. But then Barbie left, and Pemberton asked Laude if she wanted to go further. It was then that he, the US Marine stationed in the Philippines, in his own words had felt "raped." Either she told him, or he realized that she was trans. "It had a dick," Pemberton told his friend. He claimed he instinctively put Laude in an "armlock," during which she died. The autopsy of Laude's body used more technical language, determining that she had been killed by asphyxiation through strangulation.[41]

"I think I killed a he/she," Pemberton confessed to his fellow soldier.[42]

On this basis, the Philippines National Police were prepared to arrest Pemberton, but the US military refused to cooperate. The 1998 Visiting Forces Agreement between the two countries, a central plank of American imperialism in a former colony, granted the US jurisdiction over lawbreaking servicepeople. The US refused to give up Pemberton, provoking outrage across the Filipino political spectrum. Trans activists and Laude's family joined anticolonial demonstrators in protests demanding the end to the US military presence in the Philippines in her name. The murder of a trans woman by an American soldier became an indictment of, not to mention an allegory for, the violence of colonialism. That the US military, whose presence perpetuated a long history of sexual violence against Filipinas like Laude, would protect Pemberton from standing trial was treated as proof of the fundamental wrongness of the relationship between the two countries. "Jennifer's death is a result of continued American imperialism in the Philippines," explained Naomi Fontanos, a trans Filipina activist. "There's no denying that." Justice for Laude, in the eyes of activists and protestors, would be nothing less than justice for the Philippines. As the Laude family's lawyer, Virgie Suarez, was working on the case against Pemberton one evening, a nephew interrupted her. He asked his aunt what she meant when she said everyone wanted justice for Jennifer. Would "justice" bring Laude back to life? Suarez replied that they couldn't do that. Justice couldn't bring her back from the dead. "But if there is no justice," she told him, "not only will Jennifer be dead, but we'll all be dead."[43]

Laude may have been the target of a familiar form of violence —a trans woman murdered by a man with relative power as a US Marine. And Pemberton's use of the trans panic defense was also typical. But Laude could not be reduced to a statistic. The documentary *Call Her Ganda* (2018), which follows the efforts to see Pemberton convicted, shows a woman who was deeply loved. Laude shared a vibrant social world with other trans Filipinas who respected her as a leader. "She's the one we all listen to," one of her friends explains in Tagalog in the documentary. "She's the smartest of us. That's why we listen to her." Laude also had a fiancé from Germany whom she was planning to marry once her visa was approved. They had already picked out a wedding dress. And her family, still in mourning, was at the center of fighting in her name. Jennifer's mother, Nanay Julita Laude, opens *Call Her Ganda* with the shrine and memorial she created in her daughter's bedroom. Jennifer had moved away from their rural home to work at a beauty salon in Olongapo, one of the only professions open to trans women. "Every week, she would send me all her money," explains Nanay. "And she promised, 'Mom, when I come home, they will not make fun of me and call me a "queer" [*bakla*]. I will have accomplished something. My life has value.'" With tears streaming down her cheeks, Nanay shares that she had called Jennifer *ganda* since her childhood. The word means "beautiful" in Tagalog.

Jennifer had more than earned that name. In selfie footage shot on her phone not long before her death, *Call Her Ganda* shows Laude as a confident high femme. Strutting for the camera at a beauty pageant, she is wearing a red dress with crystal earrings that match a broach and arm bracelet. Her long hair is light brown, framing her delicately, and she smiles with a powerful grace. Laude is soft and demure to the camera, waving and blowing a kiss, but she has the unmistakable presence of so many trans women of color: earned and resplendent. Laude may have been killed because of the structuring violence of US imperialism in the Philippines, but the startling force of her femininity on camera, combined with the raw love and anger of those she left behind, makes one thing very clear: being a trans woman did not seal her fate. Her beauty was, on the contrary, a source of tremendous and unkillable power.

A few years earlier—and halfway around the world, in the country that had sent Pemberton to the Philippines—CeCe McDonald was walking to the store in her working-class Minneapolis neighborhood. It was around midnight in June—still early summer in the Midwest. Her shopping list was simple: bacon, eggs, and biscuits for breakfast the next morning. McDonald was walking with four friends, who, like her, were all in their early twenties. She had become accustomed to shopping late at night because the cloak of darkness helped attenuate the constant street harassment she had endured for years. As McDonald and her friends passed the Schooner Tavern, they were accosted by a volley of slurs hurled by a clutch of older white people drinking and smoking outside the bar.

"Faggots" jostled them out of their conversation.

An array of artless transphobic language alternating with the *n*-word followed from the lips of a white man in his forties named Dean Schmitz.[44]

McDonald was no stranger to this sort of unprovoked harassment, with its characteristic mix of indiscriminate homophobia, transphobia, and anti-Black racism. Years of endurance had made her confident and unapologetic. "I think—no, I know," she later wrote, "that if I never learned to assert myself that I would've never gained the courage to defend myself against those who have no respect or gratitude towards others in the world, [and] I would have met my demise years ago."[45]

"Excuse me," she said to Schmitz and his friends. "We are people, and you need to respect us."

The volley of vicious language only escalated. McDonald and her friends turned to start walking away.

It was then that the girlfriend of the man who had been harassing them, Molly Flaherty, yelled after them, "I'll take all of you bitches on!" She had been sipping from a tumbler glass outside the bar. Now she hit McDonald in the face with it so hard that it tore through her skin and flesh into her salivary gland, causing incredible pain. In the fight that ensued, Schmitz advanced on McDonald. She happened to have a pair of scissors on her and held them out in defense, fearing for her life. Schmitz lumbered right into them and was wounded badly enough that he later died.

Despite the fact that she had not initiated the fight, McDonald was arrested and charged with second-degree murder. And ignoring an outpouring of outrage and organizing from Black and trans activists, the local district attorney was relentless in his mission to convict McDonald for her self-defense. To avoid a potentially staggering eighty years in prison, like most people facing criminal charges in the US, McDonald took a plea deal.[46]

In the end, McDonald served nineteenth months in a men's prison in St. Cloud, Minnesota. Following the tradition of Black political prisoners, her prison letters indict the extreme criminalization that chases Black trans women. Yet she felt that incarceration was only one instance in an unending pattern of anti-Black and gendered violence in her life, "whether it be a tyrannical leader's harsh rule over a nation or domestic rule inside the household."[47] Physical violence against trans women like her was a facet of something larger and all-encompassing. "My idea," she explained in one letter, "is that when a man's ego and reputation are at stake, they fold into the pressure of society's idea of what masculin/ity is. For me, it comes off as if femininity, homosexism, or transgenderism is contagious and that the man's masculinity is jeopardized with the association of the fem-man and/or (trans)woman."[48] Men's violence against Black trans women, whether in the context of dating, street harassment, or the kind of racist attack she faced in her neighborhood, dresses itself up as retribution. It is an attempt to secure manhood against the perceived threat of femininity when it gets too close for comfort. Crucially, men pursue physical violence with certainty that the police, the courts, and the prison system will side with them. "There is nothing really in place for women to protect themselves," writes McDonald.

"We need to unite and make a voice for all those who have become victims of violence."[49]

After over a year of legal action and protest, Pemberton was eventually tried and sentenced by a Philippines court to six to ten years in prison. He was, in fact, the very first US soldier to be convicted of a crime under Philippine law. However, the judge also accepted Pemberton's trans panic defense, reducing the charge from murder to homicide. Even then, the US military refused to give him up. After the verdict, US soldiers physically surrounded Pemberton, initiating a tense courthouse standoff with police that lasted several hours. The judge eventually caved, ruling to delay Pemberton's imprisonment. He was transferred to the US-run Camp Aguinaldo military base, where he was protected for the next five years. In September 2020, the Olongapo City Regional Trial Court granted Pemberton a partial motion of reconsideration, releasing him from the prison sentence he had never served. Shortly afterward, the Philippines' far-right president, Roderigo Duterte, pardoned Pemberton for killing Laude, and he was deported to the US.[50]

Laude and McDonald are only two of the countless recent entries in the ledger of violence against trans women around the world. They were both framed by their attackers as an inherent threat to be put down violently. And in both cases the state joined ranks with their attackers. Pemberton had his charge reduced, and the US military protected him from imprisonment until he was pardoned. McDonald did time for her self-defense against a life-threatening attack. What made the violence stick, leading to campaigns for justice, was the victim-blaming that let its perpetrators off the hook, with the blessings of the state.

Laude's and McDonald's stories dramatize three key features of the subject of this book. First, trans misogyny, when it spills over into physical violence, is not only an expression of a perceived killability of trans women but part of a larger state-sponsored pattern of violence. Second, and more startlingly, their killers are often successful as a result in claiming that killing trans women is rational. Third, trans misogynist violence is interpreted as a legitimate response to a panic other people experience—and this rationale is so widely accepted that even self-defense can land trans women in prison. These features tell us that trans panic and its violence aren't merely the expression of individual hatred. If they were, the state wouldn't need to play such an active role in guaranteeing their impunity.

Trans-feminized people, regardless of how they identify or what language they speak, have been targeted and killed under similar circumstances for at least the past 150 years. But this history also shows that men don't inevitably lash out in violence. Rather than treating trans panic as a tragic inevitability, or as a psychological flaw in men, physical violence has not only a pattern but a history, too. This characteristic form of assault had to be invented, which means it can one day be overcome.

Behind the stories of Laude and McDonald sits the history of a global trans panic in which individual acts of violence followed the invitation of state power. The same logic of trans panic and its retaliatory violence was visited upon Bhoorah in the 1850s, Jennie June and Crow badés in the 1890s, and Jennifer Laude and CeCe McDonald in the twenty-first century. Even when it didn't lead to the kind of spectacular violence that includes murder, the same danger found many more trans-feminized people by the late nineteenth century, including Loop the Loop and Nancy Kelly.

Much like with Pemberton, who killed Laude in the context of the US military's continued presence in the Philippines, individual acts of violence tend to align with or benefit from a cultural, legal, and state-level trans panic. In other words, individual subjects of trans panic who attack trans-feminized people do so in an environment that encourages them to see trans femininity as simultaneously desirable and threatening, whether or not they are officially acting in the name of the state (as police or soldiers do). Interpersonal violence forms part of a history of state violence against trans femininity.

Still, to put it this way only explains how violence against trans women operates from one scale to another. It has not yet answered why it does so. Feminist critics like Julia Serano, Talia Mae Bettcher, Kate Manne, and Jacqueline Rose have suggested that trans women are mistreated for the same reason that many other kinds of women are mistreated: to punish them for stepping out of the lines of patriarchy. But that explanation only works if "trans women" are a distinct and unified group being punished for not living up to the ideal of womanhood. That might explain the violence that Laude and McDonald experienced in the twenty-first century, since both of them understood themselves to be trans women. But the global trans panic suggests a more complicated story that begins with far less discriminate violence against entire populations like hijras, badé, and fairies. The consistent sexualization of entire groups as male sodomites might make it seem like they are being punished for failing to conform to womanhood—except none of them considered themselves to be women in the first place. This suggests that trans panic and, indeed, trans misogyny are much less discriminate than contemporary identity politics might suggest. Trans-feminizing violence, historically speaking, probably ran ahead of most people identifying as trans women. Clearly someone like Jennie June, or possibly Loop the Loop, was an early adopter of trans womanhood as a lens through which to understand how they were different from both generic women and queer men. But hijras and the Crow badés were not destined to think of themselves as trans women. Neither was Nancy Kelly, who went on to live a happy life as a Black gay man. Trans misogyny, as a pattern of violence, exceeds trans womanhood in its scope. In the global trans panic, the target of trans-feminization was not trans women narrowly, but people who appeared to the state as feminine but were classified as male.

Exploring the implications of this conclusion begs the question of why the otherwise-different scenes of trans-feminization described in this chapter all revolve around labor and public space. As the next chapter explores, trans-feminized people's ways of life reformed in the wake of the displacement and disruption of the global trans panic. The historical experience of hijras, who were first accused of being prostitutes and then were forced into sex work by the colonial states, offers a key clue. Trans misogyny has not manifested exclusively as harassment or physical violence against trans women; it also structures and limits the ways of life to which trans-feminized people have access, often by pushing them into informal economies to survive.

The history of trans panic, in other words, generates another question: Why do trans women do sex work?

Depending on who you ask, the trans woman sex worker might be a mere stereotype. Or her job might be an unfortunate product of deprivation, as it often is in anti-sex-work feminism. Trans women would do a wide range of work, according to such arguments, but they cannot because transphobia in the labor force remains an obstacle. In this view, sex work is perhaps a last resort for trans women, just as it's seen as the last resort of all women down on their luck. These anti-sex-work answers all presume that doing sex work somehow degrades or sullies trans women from lives they otherwise were destined to lead.[51] Trans womanhood is, accordingly, made respectable when it's stripped of labor and money. Yet people still line up to pay trans women for sex, or to watch them in porn. Those two transactions are widely perceived to be how many non-trans people, especially straight men, form their first relationship to trans womanhood.

When it comes to answering these questions, trans women themselves aren't nearly as evasive as the men who jerk off to them under the covers at night or who pay them for blowjobs in their cars—or as the liberal feminists who want to rescue them from sex work to prove their value. Many have spoken with great sophistication when asked. In ethnographic research with Black trans sex workers in Chicago, Julian Kevon Glover stresses that they "have numerous work options and engage in sex work by situating their labor in the sexual economy alongside, rather than outside, other types of work." Adding sex work to other kinds of labor, these Black trans women were most like the non-trans Black women in their lives, rather than standing apart from them.[52] Taking up sex work as a form of "self-investment," Black trans women may have a higher price tag than many attached to their needs and desires, but they refused to exceptionalize their situations. "I look at everything in my life as customer service," explained Shayna, one of Glover's informants. "Because if you want me to do anything for you, I'm giving you my customer service."[53]

How long has customer service been the predominant condition of women like Shayna? Turning back the clock two hundred years, to a moment when wage labor itself was new, it becomes clear that sex work has long been pivotal and complex for its trans woman practitioners.

For Europeans or Americans contemplating living as women in the nineteenth century, giving up recognition as a man meant transition was primarily a loss of status and wealth. On the female side of the gender line, neither of the two prevailing contracts available to non-trans women—marriage or unskilled labor—were there to cushion the dramatic fall. Both demanded a degree of passing that was difficult to maintain over a lifetime. Besides, as wage labor came to dominate the global economy, simply to be an unmarried working woman was already an impoverished life. Little remained for unmarriageable trans women other than the lowest-paid service work, whether dancing in a bar, performing onstage, or selling sex. These services were patronized by growing populations of working men with a little money to spend. From the perspective of moral reformers, or the police, "public women" were all guilty of prostitution, regardless of what they did for money. Understanding trans womanhood as a way of life built into the modern service economy goes a long way toward explaining its enduring relationship to sex work. And one of the first in a long line of Black trans women like Shayna to make that connection pay, despite immense personal risk, was known as Mary Jones.

2

Sex and the Antebellum City

One June evening in 1836, a stonemason named Robert Haslem was out walking the streets, like countless other New Yorkers. The antebellum city revolved around what today is called Lower Manhattan, and it was best experienced as a pedestrian. Two marquee avenues—Broadway on the west and the Bowery on the east—flanked a sociable urban environment without many rivals. The elite lived in lavish mansions only blocks from working-class row houses, the docks lining the rivers, and the notorious slum Five Points. There was no single segregated neighborhood for the city's sizable free Black population. And vice, for which New York was world renowned, was for sale just about everywhere. Instead of confining themselves to a red-light district, brothels and houses of assignation played neighbor to fancy hotels, reputable theaters, and working-class homes. Visitors to the country's largest city often remarked that Broadway, America's answer to the Champs-Élysées, was the place to be seen, not just for wealthy white people but for stylish Black dandies and flamboyant sex workers, too. Everyone seemed to rub shoulders in New York. And these intimacies across social hierarchies of race, class, and gender seemed to be causing more tension with each passing year.

As a white man with a semi-skilled job, Haslem had a city full of entertainment and pleasure at his fingertips. He wandered a couple of blocks West from the Bowery onto Bleecker Street, where he passed an impeccably dressed Black woman also out strolling. Her teardrop white earrings and a gilt comb gracing her hair must have sparkled in the low sun.

"Where are you going, pretty maid?" he asked, implying he would like to join her.

Making each other's acquaintance, Haslem learned her name was Mary Jones. She threw an arm around him, and they walked together a while, making conversation. It took only ten or fifteen minutes to arrive at a row house on Greene Street, where what had been implied so far could be negotiated. Haslem wanted to pay a few dollars to have sex with Jones. They didn't go inside the house but headed around back, to the alley. What sort of sex transpired is lost to history, but as he walked home afterward, Haslem realized that his wallet was missing. In the 1830s this was cause for alarm. Many working men carried practically their life's savings in bank notes with them, a much safer idea than leaving them in a shared home. Losing your wallet could amount to financial ruin.[1] Curiously, though, there was now a wallet belonging to someone else tucked into his clothes.

Somehow, Haslem was able to track down the owner of the mysterious wallet. The two of them hardly had to guess what they had in common. Among the cautionary tales men shared about sex workers was that they liked to pickpocket unsuspecting marks. Men routinely took sex workers to court over it and often succeeded in recovering their money.[2] But New York had very few police officers, and no official municipal force. Most cops only worked during the day, leaving the city to private night watchmen after dark. Considering the hour, Haslem and his gullible new friend decided to wait until morning to act. The officer they found the next day, named Bowyer, suggested he should try to catch Jones in the act again, when he would arrest her.

That evening, as the sun set, Bowyer set out in plain clothes on the Bowery, strolling until he saw someone matching the suspect's description. Sure enough, it was Jones.

"Where are you going at this time of night?" he asked her. "I am going home," she replied. "Will you go, too?"

They walked to the Greene Street house and went inside, where Bowyer made himself out to be a bit of a strange client. He said he didn't want to have sex in her room. No, he wanted to go out to the alley around back. Jones assented and they relocated. In the alley she again signaled they could get intimate, but instead of returning her invitation, he tried to restrain her. As Jones struggled with him, several wallets fell out of her bosom —and one of them was Haslem's. Bowyer arrested her on the spot. While she was detained, he searched her room inside, finding more wallets. But when he went to search Jones's person, he found something he hadn't expected. His suspect, a stylish Black woman who fit in perfectly among the city's many streetwalkers, was apparently male.

Six days later, Mary Jones was tried for grand larceny in the Court of General Sessions. She pleaded not guilty but was convicted and sentenced to prison.[3]

Or so goes this version of events—a composite of coverage in the city's scandal-obsessed penny press. It was so well crafted that many of the details are hard to trust and even harder to verify. How could Jones have been so sloppy as to replace Haslem's wallet with another man's? How did Haslem find that other man? How did the police officer, whose name sounded oddly like the avenue where he met Jones, convince her to go into the alley without raising her suspicions? And wasn't it a bit too convenient that a bunch of wallets should have fallen out of Jones's bosom at the precise moment of the plot's climax? One or two of those details might be plausible on their own, but altogether they sounded more like journalistic fiction than fact, which would hardly have been unusual in the penny press. Does that mean the accusation that Jones was "a man" was also false?[4]

While many unbelievable details swirled around Mary Jones's arrest in 1836, that she was trans in an antebellum sense was not hard to establish: she said it herself, under oath. Municipal records for antebellum criminal cases were short and handwritten. The Court of General Sessions was not well funded and rarely called on lawyers. Trials were swift and justice shallow, with the presiding court officer exercising an overwhelming degree of power. As a result, the trial record for *People v. Sewally* (Jones's legal surname) is only three pages long. Its brevity makes for far less salacious reading than the columns that ran in the *New York Sun* and the *Herald*. Most of it inventories the stolen property: Haslem's wallet (worth fifty cents), ninety-nine dollars in "various bank bills" (the most common way at the time to carry money), and some "omnibus stage tickets" worth another two dollars. The total value translates to around $3,200 today.[5]

A single page records Jones's testimony in court. The scribe summarized most of her declarations, meaning not all of it was intended to be verbatim. And considering Jones was a free Black woman appearing in court less than ten years after New York State had abolished slavery, her voice was mediated by the incredulity of white interlocutors.[6] Her testimony began with establishing that she was thirty-two years old, had been born in the city, and that she made "a living by cooking, waiting etc.," residing "at No. 108 Green St.," the brothel where she allegedly took Haslem. After being asked her "right name" and replying "Peter Sewally. I am a man," Jones was asked: "What induced you to dress yourself in Women's Clothes?" Her answer formed the single longest piece of testimony recorded. "I have been in the practice of waiting upon girls of ill-fame and made the Beds and received the Company at the door and received the money for the Rooms etc," she said. "And they induced me to dress in women's clothes, saying I looked so much better in them and I have always attended parties among the people of my own Colour dressed in that way—and in New Orleans I always dressed in this way."

The rest of the trial record runs only a few more sentences. When asked if she stole Haslem's wallet, she answered emphatically. "No Sir and I never saw the gentleman nor laid eyes upon him. I threw no Pocket Book from my coat the last night, and had none to throw away." The record does not explain the reasoning of the court's conclusion, let alone the jury's, nor does it list a sentence. But the penny press did, spinning a bit of theater out of the whole affair. The *Sun* emphasized that despite being forced to give her legal name, Jones appeared in court "neatly dressed in feminine attire, and his head covered with a female wig." This was meant to play for laughs, as it apparently had in court. The *Herald* reported "the greatest merriment" at Jones's courtroom entrance, "and his Honor the Recorder, the sedate grave Recorder laughed till he cried." If the image of a judge in stitches wasn't enough, the *Sun* added that someone in the court's gallery, "seated behind the prisoner's box, snatched the flowing wig from the head of the prisoner," prompting another "tremendous roar of laughter throughout the room."[7]

The comedic mise en scène is hard to take at face value, but it served a purpose. Jones became a lasting sensation in the press. The cause of her infamy wasn't that she was really a man under her women's clothing; rather, the satire of her clothes and wig had to do with her being free and Black. "Sewally has for a long time past been doing a fair business," the *Herald* reported, "both in money making, and *practical amalgamation*, under the cognomen of *Mary Jones*."[8] The phrase "practical amalgamation," not the putative mismatch between her womanhood and her body, was the scandal. There were thousands of sex workers in New York, many working openly in the city's streets. Only two months prior, the details of the commercial sex industry were given public airing at the murder trial of Richard P. Robinson, accused of killing a young white sex worker named Helen Jewett.[9] What made Jones different was that she openly sold sex across the color line. Not long after the trial, a lithograph of Jones captioned "The Man-Monster" began to appear around Manhattan, pasted in shop windows and on brick buildings. In the illustration, Jones is the very picture of refined elegance. Wearing a fashionable gown of blue flowers cinched in a high waist, delicate white gloves, stockings, and earrings, her look could have arrived on the latest ship from Paris. She is poised like an elite woman, holding a purse in one hand and a man's pocketbook in the other (no doubt a wink to the trial). Her expression is serene and confident, and she locks eyes directly with the viewer. The caption offers a few choice details from her trial: "Peter Sewally, alias Mary Jones. Sentenced 18th June 1836 to 5 years imprisonment at hard labor at Sing Sing for Grand Larceny."[10]

The conventionally fashionable portrait of Jones was intended, like the *Sun*'s riff on her appearance in court, to read as derogatory for white readers. It was not a caricature of a mismatched gender, except incidentally, as part of a racial satire. The sheer pretension of a free Black woman strolling the city like a white woman signaled her real duplicity, inviting mockery. By fitting in too well, or passing fashionably in a way that undermined the hierarchy between white and Black New Yorkers, Jones was made a symbol of "practical amalgamation," or interracial sex. The fact that she literally sold sex only sealed the deal. The details of her case, including her being trans, were mere superlatives. Jones became famous because her public presence and line of work were twisted to satirize abolitionism in a decade where white supremacists were training their eyes on the city's free Black population. If *this* was how free Black New Yorkers lived, daring to consider themselves equal to white people in all matters, the fact that behind their fine clothing and deportment lay sex work was all the proof needed that the national abolition of slavery would inevitably lead to the "amalgamation" of the races. That may have been a white supremacist fantasy, but it had already produced real effects. The year 1834 had been marked by violent pro-slavery riots in New York, led by seething white mobs.

The presentation of Jones's trial as a satire of abolition also makes the archival record nearly impossible to trust. Other than the trial record, which contains few details, she exists primarily *as a joke* in the lithograph, the antebellum press, and the occasional crime writer's reference.[11] Although her testimony in court established that she was trans in some sense, almost everything else written about her was the fantasy, punchline, or wholesale invention of a white author. Among the worst of those inventions was the nickname "beefsteak Pete." The *Sun* originated the moniker in its trial coverage, but it was repeated for years by papers whenever Jones was again arrested, usually for vagrancy—a charge typically levied at sex workers, as well as free Black residents of the city.[12] The euphemism "beefsteak Pete" suggested that Jones used some sort of leather device to simulate female genitals in her work. Careful not to risk an obscenity prosecution, the *Sun* gave its explanation of the contraption in horrendous Latin. It translates literally—and awkwardly—as saying that Jones "had been fitted with a piece of cow pierced and opened like a woman's womb, held up with a girdle."[13]

The fact that the *Sun* mixed up the vagina with the womb (and "cow" with leather) is only one of many reasons not to believe the story. It's hard to fathom that the court would have ignored something related to her dress and work, although Jones was not on trial for sodomy, sex work, or any sexual offense at all. Neither prostitution nor interracial sex were illegal in New York, and sodomy prosecutions were extremely rare, being almost impossible to prove.[14] It's more likely that the *Sun* invented the beefsteak to up the ante of the libel against free Black New Yorkers *and* white abolitionists. New York's reputation as a place where high society shared the streets with fallen sex workers and Black dandies was a powerful white supremacist metaphor. As performance studies scholar Tavia Nyong'o puts it, "the caricature here cuts both ways: certainly against Sewally but also against well-to-do ladies and gentlemen attempting French pretensions along Broadway." The penny press was "casting impolite doubts as to whether or not 'Mr. Robert Haslem' was in fact deceived" by Jones at all, "or whether indeed gender had not become stylized beyond recognition within the flux of urban life."[15] What was spectacular about Mary Jones was, once again, not that she was a trans woman but rather that she was a free Black woman whose gender was already construed as so much trickery. The joke was not only that she passed herself off as a respectable woman when she was really a sex worker, but that the respectable white men and women who rubbed shoulders with her might be just as fake by association. That is what the loaded phrase "practical amalgamation" was designed to convey. As Nyong'o explains, "the modifier 'practical' redoubles the satire insofar as it indexes the standard antiabolitionist charge that equality *in theory* meant amalgamation *in practice*. Sewally's activities were thus obliquely produced as evidence against the claims of abolitionists, as indexing the social chaos that would accompany the overthrow of slavery and racial domination."[16] The beefsteak was a salacious plot point in pressing that case, functioning like an allegory for the unnaturalness of interracial sex that would result from legal equality, rather than an explanation of how trans women had sex. If Haslem was tricked by Jones and almost lost everything, so, too, would white people be tricked and ruined by the duplicity of free Black people if slavery were to end nationally. It hardly mattered whether the piece of leather existed, or what Jones's anatomy really looked like. Her dress and earrings were already suspect. *Everything* about free Black womanhood was sexualized and ridiculed by the antebellum white public.

But if the archive concerning Jones is so untrustworthy, then what can Jones say to trans history? If she wasn't singled out for being trans but was satirized for being a free Black woman, what difference does it makes? And what does her life explain about the relationship between trans womanhood and sex work? To answer these questions without falling back into the realm of racial satire, Jones left behind only one piece of evidence. In one line in her testimony at trial, she smuggled in a clue for telling her story differently: "I have always attended parties among the people of my own Colour dressed in that way —and in New Orleans I always dressed in this way."

In the closest thing to her own words, Mary Jones did not perceive her way of life to be exceptional. Rather, her trans womanhood was part of the fabric of Black life in New York City and New Orleans. That her assertion survives two centuries later is astounding. She had already answered the court's question about why she wore women's clothing with a story as old as modern trans femininity: the women she worked with at the Greene Street brothel told her she looked better dressed as a woman, so she kept it up. That same cover story would recur among trans women in the Victorian era and well into the twentieth century.[17] Why, then, did she also emphasize being at home among Black people? Why mention New Orleans at all? Indeed, the references were irrelevant to the legal proceedings. Jones was not arrested for cross-dressing, nor did geography figure into the case. Perhaps something in her delivery convinced the court to record that part of her testimony. Whatever the reason, treating this line as historical evidence quickly runs aground on its brevity. Where does a single sentence spoken in 1836 lead? Black feminist historians of slavery and its afterlives have developed powerful methods of rigorous speculation to work with moments of extreme incompleteness in the record—tools that cultural historian Saidiya Hartman, for instance, calls "critical fabulation," and historian Marisa Fuentes calls "reading along the bias grain" of archival documents.[18] Following their methodology, what if Jones was communicating something urgent that stands apart from the rest of the trial record when she referred to Black social life in New York and New Orleans? How would her story have to shift to accommodate the fullest possibilities embedded in her testimony?

Jones surfaces today as an impressively early example of modern Black trans women's history—not to mention evidence of sex work as modern trans women's oldest profession. But to escape the distorting satire that immortalized her in the press, we must explain two key facets of her life: her membership in a free Black community during US slavery, and her profession as a sex worker when wage labor had not yet replaced all forms of work. Put differently, it can hardly be a coincidence that a Black trans woman's way of life should have arisen in an era animated by tensions between slavery and emancipation, or between urban wage labor and urban sex work. And it cannot be a coincidence that a free Black woman would exploit the paradoxes of antebellum mobility to find a concretely trans way in the world.

In naming trans womanhood "a way of life," this telling of Mary Jones's story lets go entirely of any question about her identity. The point of studying Jones is hardly to define what a Black trans woman is and then pin it on the past, or vice versa. It would strain reason to imagine she thought of herself as having or expressing an inner identity nearly two hundred years ago. To be a self-possessed individual with a trans identity is not only an incredibly recent phenomenon; it's one that would have been quite alien to a free Black woman in the antebellum era. Building on the last chapter's concept of trans-feminization as a condition imposed by the state on entire populations, this chapter argues that sex work emerged for trans-feminized people as one of their only viable ways of life. Chapter 1 focused on a slightly later moment in time, in colonial India. There, the *hijra* ascetic way of life was materially disrupted by the British colonial state, eventually forcing hijras into sex work when criminalization and police harassment had deprived them of their prior ways of earning a living. It was through this process that hijras were indiscriminately trans-feminized as a class, instead of being recognized for being trans women by Western criteria. This chapter raises another circumstance where trans means something like a dilemma of how to live in the aftermath of state-sponsored dispossession, or trans-feminization at the population level. In Jones's case, dispossession was as old and vast as the transatlantic slave trade.

Black womanhood had been so intensely unmade over centuries under chattel slavery that what was trans about Jones is inseparable from the story of Black gender during the incomplete transition from plantation slavery to industrial capitalism. The economic and social mobility that came with emancipation in New York was just enough to let Jones transform Black womanhood into something livable by doing sex work. But that condition of possibility was undercut by a host of national and international forces. If we dig deeper into the free Black community and antebellum sex work, we see how difficult but potentially rewarding Black trans womanhood as a way of life was to achieve against its two primary alternatives: enslavement or dependence on a man in marriage. Jones's testimony to the naturalness of her way of life in the Black Atlantic world is a portal to a life caught between extreme unfreedom, the commandment to become a different kind of property in marriage, and the hollow promise of capitalist freedom to work for wages—or end up in prison, as she would many times.

Jones was born in 1803. Four years earlier, New York state had passed the Gradual Emancipation Law, a conservative form of abolition granting children born to an enslaved mother eventual freedom. There's no way to be certain, but Jones may have been born free (if her mother already was). At trial in 1836 she mentioned being born in the city, but not into bondage or indenture. If she had been born into slavery, or ever captured and forced into it for a time, she had little reason to tell the court. Still, while many enslaved Black residents of New York emancipated themselves and their family during her youth—usually by purchasing their freedom—those transactions produced records that might have come up during a criminal trial. Jones mentions having been in "the service"—a state militia, perhaps—but nothing else about her past. In 1817 New York passed a second law accelerating the gradual emancipation schedule, meaning that no matter her prior condition, she would have been free at the latest on July 4, 1827.[19]

Whether born free or emancipated, Jones was part of a monumental generation experiencing Black freedom as their predominant condition. By the time she was arrested in 1836, it was precisely her publicity as a free Black woman for which the press pursued her so viciously. The city's population was exploding as industrialization and the expansion of American slavery in the South flooded New York's port with cotton and money. In 1830 the city was home to 200,000 people, an increase of over sixty percent in one decade. Nearly 14,000 of them were free and Black. And because women had outnumbered men during legal slavery, the free Black population still tilted female. It was also richly diverse in origin: unlike Jones, most were born elsewhere. The Caribbean, including the free Black nation of Haiti, had supplied a steady stream of immigrants for decades. Now, as the Southern cotton economy moved westward to the Mississippi valley, it pushed many, including runaway slaves, north to New York. The city was a beacon, but it was far from safe. Slave catchers, many willing to kidnap anyone they could make fit a description, lurked in its neighborhoods.[20]

The spirit of emancipation—and its fragility—made for a bold free Black community. Black churches popped up throughout New York, and the first Black theater opened in 1821, daring to debut a formerly enslaved actor in the Shakespearean role of Richard III. The free Black population had a reputation for the flashiest styles, the sharpest tongues, and trendsetting music and dance. Whether it took the form of envy or resentment, Black people's confidence in public was interpreted by white onlookers as a powerful assertion. "The stroll," or walking the streets, marked free Black New Yorkers as defiant in the short era prior to urban segregation. Otherwise, the street was the place they worked. Selling and serving food, street cleaning, and other extremely low-paid jobs were about all free Black people could get—and even then, those jobs were far easier for men to come by than women. By the 1830s some kinds of labor, like selling oysters, were considered a specifically Black line of work.[21]

Any illusion that abolition would lead to economic equality was dashed by this point. Being restricted to the lowest-paid jobs made an already expensive, overstuffed city of predatory real estate speculators tougher for free Black New Yorkers than anyone else. By the 1830s, organized labor was openly pitting white men against Black men, feeding into riots of 1834. More broadly, white New Yorkers resented that their Black neighbors dared to live any differently from the era of slavery—an absurd expectation but for the stranglehold of racism. As a hub of Black freedom, New York simmered with local tensions, but it was also a magnet in the national and international battle over American slavery. Jones's trial was one spark in a raging blaze.[22]

In this context, it's not hard to imagine why sex work was appealing to Jones. Whatever her military stint amounted to, it implies she had tried to make it as a man at least once. But the downward mobility of living as a woman was ironically minimal on top of the economic situation of free Black workers after emancipation. By choosing to live as a woman, Jones was hardly forgoing a lucrative career as a street cleaner or oyster vendor. However she got her start, by living in a brothel and doing domestic work in addition to streetwalking she was a fairly typical sex worker. And she was in good company. The explosion in the city's sex economy tracks with the surge in its population and the money brought by industrialization. New York had become a city of bankers, businessmen, and proletarians. The last group—by far the largest—was defined by having no property but their bodies, forced to sell their labor. Wages, along with the transient urban population to whom they were paid, fed the development of commercialized leisure on a mass scale for the first time, including sex.[23] In the 1820s the number of brothels swelled throughout the city. Five Points may have had the worst reputation, but the Greene Street row house in which Jones lived and worked was almost a mile north. Landlords, who were making money hand over fist off a housing shortage, could demand some of the highest rents from sex workers in return for protection. This tidy arrangement between the sexual underground and the city elite characterized the antebellum era. Sex was for sale everywhere in New York, and few people, except for moral reformers, wanted to curb it.[24]

Sex work was overwhelmingly a woman's profession. Like Jones, it tended to attract women who were unable to fulfill the moral imperatives that defined the American nineteenth century: the cult of true womanhood and separate-spheres ideology. As cities like New York ballooned into the largest the country had ever seen, insistence on a stark division between public and private space was one way to manage the numeric threat of angry workers suffering under the unprecedented brutality of industrialism. By dint of the gendered line between public and private, women and girls could be confined to the home, not simply chaste but economically subordinate to husbands and fathers. Men, in turn, relied on steady work to support their entire family, making it harder to risk organizing against their bosses. Still, for most women this arrangement was a cheap fiction. The proletarianized European immigrants arriving by ship in New York Harbor couldn't afford private space to confine themselves to, surviving instead in overcrowded housing. Nor could they avoid working. For free Black New Yorkers, who inherited nothing but legal freedom through emancipation, the situation was even more pointed. By the time Mary Jones started streetwalking, being trans was only one in a long line of reasons why getting married wasn't a viable economic path in life.[25]

New York's sex workers tended to be young, unmarried women supplementing poorly paid jobs, like sewing or domestic work. The most common reason they got started was the death of a working male relative or another poverty-triggering event. Many only worked casually and for a few years, hoping the money they made would translate into upward mobility, or even marriage to a client. It rarely did; only a few white madams got rich turning sex work into a business. Still, sex work in New York was a women-run industry. There were no pimps, and women owned and operated most of the commercial infrastructure. Even those at the bottom of the hierarchy, the streetwalkers, were esteemed by the public for their autonomy. Yet self-sufficiency was, paradoxically, the same reason that few sex workers could ever make it: they were devalued for being women, and free Black women most of all. A seamstress in the 1830s could expect to make between $0.36 and $1.12 a week sewing shirts, while a domestic worker might bring in one to two dollars. A sex worker could make that much in a single day, but her expenses were much higher. Brothel rent ran between three and ten dollars a week, and that was before considering the clothes and styling needed to stay fashionable. Sarah Williams, a free Black sex worker, charged her clients a flat rate of just two dollars in 1835.[26] Ultimately, then, all service work for women—whether as a seamstress, domestic worker, or sex worker—paid poorly. Capitalist New York City was making its industrialists, bankers, and elites rich, not its workers, whether they toiled in the formal or informal economy. The line between the two was governed by gender and race.

Just how many of the city's sex workers were trans? There's no way to be certain, since most trans women either blended in for self-protection or were too poor to leave historical evidence behind. Jones wasn't immortalized in the press because she was trans, after all, but because of the sexual politics of abolition, making it somewhat of an accident that the historical record describes her trans womanhood. Yet there is evidence that she was not alone. Around the time she returned to the city from her prison sentence, the penny press that had made her famous had a new rival, dubbed the flash press. Aimed at "sporting men" like Robert Haslem, these papers cost more but promised riveting gossip focused on theater, sports, and sex work. They passed themselves off as organs of moral outrage, but that cover was a wink to their male readers, who used flash papers as practical guides to the underworld.[27]

In 1842, the *Whip* ran a series denouncing local sodomites, which toed the line between condemnation and providing information on exactly where and who to visit for a good time. Eight alleged sodomites were named, and the paper demanded that such "monsters" be run out of town. Some of the accused were parodied for their "feminine ... manners," but that charge emulated an old European tradition of accusing elites of sexual duplicity to dramatize their corrupt power. The *Whip* warned that "young men of rather genteel address" gathered nightly near City Hall Park, making the area "a second Palais Royale," a section of Paris notorious since the revolutionary era for blending illicit sex and corrupt aristocracy. The paper also blamed sodomy on actors, an association imported from London. But one of the eight accused sodomites was treated differently from the rest.[28]

Sally Binns, for one thing, had a woman's name and was a sex worker. The *Whip* referred to her as a man to emphasize the irony. But it then told readers exactly where to find her and how much she charged, streetwalking "on the 'four shilling side' of Broadway." Interestingly, the column also described her fashion—something it normally reserved for celebratory articles about women sex workers. Binns had hair "curled down his neck; he straddles as he walks and if anyone speaks to him, he drops a curtsy." No doubt many did speak to her if she was out streetwalking on Broadway. Relating her to the other sodomites it denounced, the *Whip* explained that Binns "puts on female attire and enacts feminine parts in the Thespian Association over St. John's Hall, in Frankfort Street." But unlike most actors, she chose to stay in the feminine role outside the theater. "Binns wears a snuff colored frock, and fashionable pantaloons, with watch, rings, and *bijouterie*," continued the profile. "He has lost all sense and feeling of manhood," in the paper's opinion. As a result, she was "not quite a woman; by no means a man."[29]

Binns was surely white, since the *Whip* was too emphatically racist in its depictions of Black people to miss an opportunity. It's remarkable not just that her streetwalking resembled Mary Jones, but that the press distinguished her from the other sodomites it denounced: while the men were lampooned through libels of aristocratic corruption, she was written up like one of the paper's darling prostitute profiles. In other words, despite its denunciation, the *Whip* profiled Binns as a woman, not a man. The reference to a theater is also telling. Perhaps the theater was a regular entry into white trans womanhood for those who desired it. On a practical level, learning to dress, do makeup, and pass as a woman would be much safer to develop onstage first. And the leap from acting to sex work could transpire inside the theater itself. Antebellum theaters reserved the "third tier," the highest balcony, for sex workers, who attended with clients or to pick them up. It wasn't so much an open secret as a well-known fact of life in the city. The *Whip* published guides to the different theaters around town and practically taught readers how to hire a sex worker.[30]

The New York theater scene was modeled on London's, down to the sex work architecture, and the occasional story of someone like Binns appeared across the Atlantic, too. In 1830, a young Irish woman named Lavinia Edwards moved into a flat with her "sister" Maria near the Coburg Theatre. Lavinia and Maria, who weren't really sisters, both had dreams of acting. Lavinia never seemed to land a gig, but she confidently told everyone that she had gotten her break acting somewhere "in the provinces." During the winter of 1833, she fell ill and was attended by a doctor but died suddenly. An inquest was ordered to rule out foul play, and the pathologist at Guy's Hospital was surprised to learn in the process that she was apparently "male." The autopsy also suggested she had an inflamed liver, which may have made her susceptible to the lung infection that killed her. Either way, foul play seemed unlikely, but an investigation ensued. Neither Maria, the attending doctor, nor the landlady claimed to have any idea Lavinia wasn't female. A local man offered the testimony that "he had seen it stated in the papers that the deceased had come from Dublin" and he used to know her. "About twelve or thirteen years ago," this man claimed, "the deceased sometimes passed as a *woman* and sometimes as a *man*." The inquest concluded she had died naturally, but, as one chronicler later put it, the jury also "expressed their horror at the unnatural conduct of the deceased, and strongly recommend the proper authorities that some means may be adopted in the disposal of the body which will mark the ignominy of the crime." This writer suggested that Lavinia's "natural appearance of effeminacy enabled him to conceal his sex with success. This, together with the fact that he was accustomed to appear on the stage in male as well as female parts, has doubtless helped him." [31]

These tales of deception would soar in number toward the end of the nineteenth century on both sides of the Atlantic as female impersonation became a type of job. The Victorian press is littered with tales of women found out to be "male," either after they died or were arrested. Many would take the first chance to skip town, starting over with a new name— even marrying several times. By the late nineteenth century, trans femininity was publicly visible enough for these sorts of stories to become part of the seedy lore of cities from London, to New York, to Chicago. In the 1830s, by contrast, Mary Jones, Sally Bins, and Lavinia Edwards were brought into the spotlight because of something initially unrelated to their trans femininity. The three had very little in common, except that they worked in the service and nightlife economy. Each of them seems to have found in trans womanhood a way of life that amplified their social and economic mobility. Edwards was a poor immigrant from colonial Ireland. Like Binns, the theater merged the possibility of living as a woman with a nightlife job. And like Jones, Binns found sex work to be one of the only ways to make enough money to purchase the autonomy she needed—until she saw her name printed in the flash press.

While histories of trans femininity stretch back much further than this period, the first few decades of the nineteenth century witnessed the growing relationships between trans womanhood, public space, and economic mobility that remain important to this day. As increasingly wage-driven economies like England and the United States were enforcing a strict gendered division of labor, women as a class were experiencing a long-term decline in their economic, social, and political power that had begun centuries earlier among peasants in Europe, and increasingly across the world through colonialism.[32] The same historical forces that had violently severed connections between people and land now flooded cities with propertyless proletarians whose ties to family and cultural traditions had been loosened by being forced to migrate to sell their labor. The possibility of sex work for those pushed into cities like New York due to colonial upheaval or the transatlantic slave trade made trans womanhood into a genuine window of opportunity. It was a chance to start over and be someone new, which would have been much harder if not for the anonymity of the city. Not that it was a form of liberation: it was more like a contradiction, where new freedoms were tied to new forms of constraint and danger, not to mention isolation.[33] While the personal feelings and beliefs of the trans women of the 1830s are impossible to reconstruct—if not irrelevant, even, to those women, given the cultural differences of the era—the economic and social currency they pursued is evident. Mary Jones's careful reference to New Orleans at her trial is the portal to the most remarkable chapter in that story.

Before exploring how she got there, it's worth emphasizing how novel it was that Mary Jones moved in a Black world stretching from New York City to New Orleans. Not only were the cities separated by a massive distance, but their organizing realities were starkly different. If New York was a relative beacon of freedom, it was so in contrast to New Orleans as the capital of what W. E. B. Du Bois would later call "the Cotton Kingdom."[34] Even when traveling with freedom papers, entering a state with legal slavery like Louisiana raised to its maximum the danger of being detained or captured. New Orleans maintained a policy of arresting all Black sailors upon arrival at the city's port, for instance. The city aimed to ensure that no enslaved person could slip through the port unaccounted for, and that no free Black person could move there without good reason.[35] In practical terms, it was a powerful demonstration of white supremacy. Black skin was the only pretext needed to arbitrarily lose one's freedom. Yet, despite such dangers, the allure of the Crescent City was undeniable. Incorporated into the United States through the Louisiana Purchase after being, successively, a French and Spanish colony, New Orleans was one of the world's major entrepôts. In less than twenty years, it went from a sleepy colonial town to the busiest outgoing port in the US, located strategically at the mouth of the Mississippi River. By 1840, New Orleans had become the third-largest city in the country, and enslaved people made up around 20 percent of its population. During this period, the city's free Black population also overtook that of all its national rivals—including New York.[36]

If there was anywhere that might draw Mary Jones from her home, it was surely New Orleans. Determining when Jones may have made a trip to New Orleans, or how many times she may have visited (if it was more than once), is extremely difficult. Consulting easily searchable ship manifests and arrival databases beginning in 1820, no obvious records belong to her, though there are many reasons the search terms themselves are doubtful. "Mary Jones" was an incredibly common name. And there's no way to be certain that she traveled under that name, or even continued using that name, as press items from later in her life refer to other aliases. There are no obvious records under her legal name given at trial, "Peter Sewally." Free Black residents of New Orleans were required to carry freedom papers, which suggests that it would have made most sense for her registered name on board or at the port to match her freedom papers; however, there are no known records of her freedom papers to consult. In a basic sense, there's no way to be sure whether she traveled dressed as a woman, as a man, or both. The choice would have affected her travel experience by ship: while free Black passengers were generally forced onto the same decks as cargo, barred from the men's and ladies' cabins, there were still relative risks for women traveling compared with those perceived to be men.

What kind of ship carried her there? The most likely answer is a schooner—a coastal sailing ship—or, depending on exactly when she traveled, a steamship.[37] By the 1820s, the steamboats later made famous by Mark Twain in *Life on the Mississippi* (1883) could make the trip upriver from New Orleans as far as Cleveland or Pittsburgh, though a rail connection on to New York didn't exist until the 1850s. From a safety perspective, picking a travel route that avoided states with legal slavery ran into a lack of infrastructure. Traveling to Pittsburgh by road to catch a steamship onward would have been slow and dangerous, stretching the total travel time to months. A coastal schooner could have brought Jones to her destination in around two weeks.[38] Still, arriving via the Gulf of Mexico was surely an ominous experience. Immigrants and travelers were outnumbered by commodities all around them. Some were dry goods from the Caribbean, or clothing and luxuries from Europe. Most were gigantic bales of cotton ending their downriver journey before continuing to New York, Massachusetts, or Liverpool. But Jones may have been most preoccupied by the human beings trafficked as commodities everywhere she looked—people whose condition was tied to the skin color she shared with them.

This isn't to say that slavery and freedom were simple opposites, or that they correlated geographically to Louisiana versus New York. The story of antebellum New Orleans and the Mississippi valley is rife with contradiction. And those contradictions structured Jones's mobility. New Orleans was home to an influential free Black community, but it was unlike the one she grew up in. Called *libres* prior to the American era, they played a characteristically Caribbean role as an intermediary class between the condition of slavery and white citizenship. When the Black revolutionaries of Saint-Domingue overthrew the French in 1790s and declared the free nation of Haiti in 1804, the elite slaveholding class fled the island. Some 10,000 of them ended up in New Orleans. Around a third were white, while another third were free people of color, and the rest were claimed by both groups as enslaved property. This influx founded the city's visible Creole community. After the US formally ended its international slave trade in 1808, the internal movement of enslaved people further transformed the city and region. Between the 1820s and 1860s, up to a million enslaved people were forcibly relocated to the Mississippi valley from other parts of the country. New Orleans maintained the single largest slave market in the South at its peak. On any given day, thousands of people might be imprisoned for sale just blocks from the levee where ships docked.[39]

The sheer number of people and goods passing through meant that Black mobility was never strictly organized by a clean division between slavery and freedom. Free Black men accounted for somewhere around a fifth of all sailors aboard American ships, meaning they were no strangers to the city.[40]

The steamships traveling up and down the Mississippi were also powered by both free and enslaved Black labor. Tracing this network, the historian Walter Johnson emphasizes the intricate connections between those aboard steamships and those who labored by the river, on the edges of plantations. Information and people, like cotton, moved much quicker than they had in prior generations. The very journey that cotton and capital took created new possibilities for what Johnson terms "the contingency—the agony—of solidarity" between the river's Black travelers. For fugitives trying to escape captivity, or a mother seeking word of her child sold upriver, "it was less an achieved state than a continual terrified request: Can you help me? Do you know the way? Will you share what you have? Will you risk your life to save mine?"[41] This was the intensely personal scale of the symbiotic relationship between slavery and capitalism. The white working-class seamstresses of New York and London made shirts out of the cotton picked, processed, and shipped by enslaved and free Black labor in the Mississippi valley. That entanglement made industrialists, bankers, and white elites rich. All of them relied on Black labor, whether free or coerced. Every relative degree of mobility in this violent economy was shot through with contradiction. No fates were equal, but all were entwined.[42]

This is where a specifically trans thread of Black mobility emerges and why Mary Jones's trip to New Orleans is so important. Black feminists have described the pivotal "ungendering" of enslaved Africans. In "Mama's Baby, Papa's Maybe: An American Grammar Book," Hortense Spillers understands the theft of bodies and souls—the experience of capture and captivity in West African ports, followed by the extreme violence of the Middle Passage—to have made millions otherwise different in language, culture, religion, and gender newly indistinguishable. Through the infliction of extreme brutality that destroyed their prior identities, enslaved Africans were made exchangeable through a common rate as commodities. "Under these conditions," explains Spillers, "we lose at least gender difference in the outcome, and the female body and the male body become a territory of cultural and political maneuver, not at all gender-related, gender specific."[43] In the Americas, the liquidation of kinship bonds, including different systems of gender, was enforced through the legal condition of being property. Marriage between enslaved people was illegal, and the patriarchal European convention of descent was broken in the doctrine of *partus sequitur ventrem* ("that which is born follows the womb"). A child born to an enslaved mother was likewise enslaved, regardless of the father's status, yet the mother retained no legal bond to her child. These institutions repeatedly severed social differences to prioritize fungibility, and Spillers reads among their many outcomes being symbolically "unmade"—a situation inherited by Black women long after formal abolition.[44]

Historians like Jennifer L. Morgan have textured Spillers's account, pointing out that despite the primacy of economic fungibility, European slave traders still made distinctions between male and female captives, especially concerning women's potential to reproduce. And despite the Middle Passage and the many efforts to prohibit enslaved Africans from maintaining connections to their home cultures, many women managed to hold onto and reimagine prior practices, especially in child-rearing and medicine.[45] It was often in women's hands that Creolized cultural and spiritual practices were forged, blending a multitude of West African ways of being and knowing with Indigenous and colonial threads accumulated in the Americas. What Black womanhood might become in response to the violence of ungendering took root in this way.

In *Black on Both Sides: A Racial History of Trans Identity*, C. Riley Snorton proposes that in the antebellum era Black gender often appeared in movement, expertly shadowing fungibility in the market economy. Fugitive narratives, for instance, often relied on the drama of cross-dressing and passing, and it was common practice in the underground railroad to cross-dress runaways to disguise them.[46] Snorton underlines that these transitive movements through gender were conscious performances. Both enslaved and free Black people channeled the ungendered quality long enforced on them and put it toward flights of mobility that could widen the degree of freedom in their lives. What was trans about these strategies was nothing transgender by today's standards. There was no line between a Black trans way of life and the malleability associated with Black gender in general. Snorton instead describes "a kind of being in the world where gender—though biologized—was not fixed but fungible, which is to say, *revisable within blackness.*"[47]

Snorton names Mary Jones as one antebellum practitioner of this sort of revision. *Black on Both Sides* also adds Mary Ann Waters, another antebellum sex worker, who was arrested in Baltimore in 1851 after the passage of the federal Fugitive Slave Act. In a pickup notice—an advertisement published when an alleged runaway had been detained—she is described as "a Negro Man, who calls himself Mary Ann Waters." According to the notice, Waters proclaimed that she was free, twenty-eight years old, and had been born not far from Baltimore. The notice described her physical features, including a scar, but also the "blue velvet mantilla, white satin bonnet, and figured scarf" in which she was arrested. According to the notice, Waters "has been hiring out in the city of Baltimore as a woman for the last three years." Snorton stresses that this short notice cannot be made to say whether Mary Ann Waters was really a free Black person or a fugitive, much like it cannot be forced to say if she was "really" trans, or "merely" in disguise. Like Jones, sex work may have been both an attempt to hide and the reason she was arrested. The point is that the various possible truths were conjoined from the very beginning. The mess of contrary meanings is likely how Mary Ann Waters experienced them, too. The ungendering of Black womanhood made possible the relative mobility of someone raised male living as a woman by doing sex work, for Black gender was precisely treated as rearrangeable. Yet the same suspicion attached to Black gender's malleability could just as plausibly have been weaponized against Waters as proof she must have been keeping a secret—not that she was trans but that she was a fugitive.[48]

Likewise, for Jones, traveling between New York City and New Orleans was not a simple matter of freedom papers granting mobility. Success in the journey would have relied on the entanglement of Black gender with both fungibility and fugitivity.

There are no obvious archival traces of Jones's trip—or trips —to New Orleans, so it falls to the method of critical fabulation to describe what might have been. She probably avoided the hot and mosquito-riven summer months, when the city emptied out some to avoid the yellow fever that came with the rain. As her ship pulled up to the levee on the Mississippi River, she might have gazed out at hundreds of other ships dotting its banks, many stuffed to their smokestacks with 400-pound bales of cotton. Like other visitors, she might have been struck from the moment she stepped off the ship by the intense diversity of the people around her. French as much as English would have filled the air, with the occasional interlude in mostly Cuban Spanish. Indigenous people, especially Chocktaw affected by President Andrew Jackson's vicious colonial policy, were common in public, as were free Black and enslaved residents, many with Caribbean styles of speech.[49] Food and other everyday items from Latin America were for sale in markets, along with the latest fashions from Paris and American goods Jones was probably used to seeing in New York. But the city itself rumbled with a growth all its own. What had once been spacious residential neighborhoods the French called *faubourgs* were fast becoming dense as wooden buildings were torn down and replaced with bricks. Elaborate hotels were under construction for wealthy tourists. Paved streets, a modern sewer system, gas lighting, and indoor water and plumbing were hallmarks of this frenzied era, establishing amenities rare in the Southern states.[50]

New Orleans was regarded by many observers as driven by competition between the American Quarter and the French Quarter. But on the back end of the French Quarter lay Congo Square, an important public space for the city's Black residents. It might have drawn Jones. On Sundays, enslaved people traveled from nearby plantations to sell goods, mostly to free Black shoppers. And the Square's Black social life extended to public music and dance, proclaiming attachments to West African cultures in a way that was becoming rarer and rarer in the US. For free Black visitors or workers enjoying downtime, the American Quarter was a popular destination for drinking and nightlife. Anyone looking for sex might head to Gallatin Street, which promised houses of assignation open to free Black and enslaved residents alike, as well as to white people.[51] While the antebellum period trended in the direction of segregation, socializing across the color line was perceived as a norm, a quirk of the city's distinctive cosmopolitan culture. "Quadroon balls"—dances where light-skinned free Black women were presented to paying white men—were an antebellum adaptation of the Caribbean practice of *plaçage*. For wealthy white men who didn't want the obligations of marriage (or already had wives), meeting a young woman at a ball might be a prelude to putting her up in an apartment where she could do domestic and sexual labor for him. Free Black women were intensely identified with sex and service work by white men in a way that blurred the line between the two, whether they were wives, *placées*, or prostitutes.[52]

The sex work economy in New Orleans is often memorialized in Storyville, a red-light district that emerged at the tail end of the nineteenth century. But fifty years earlier, the city already had a reputation that rivaled New York's. The practice of professional sex work was organized quite differently, however. Sex workers rented rooms in brothels, but those buildings were

87

generally owned by white businessmen. While that reduced economic possibilities for sex workers, the appeal would still have made sense to a New Yorker. If marriage or plaçage were not viable, selling sex rivaled or exceeded any of the low-wage work available to women in a city where enslaved labor depressed wages. Sex work, after all, was not illegal. Public-order statutes criminalizing vagrancy allowed the city's few police to arrest sex workers, but an 1818 law exacted just a month in prison, and only if a twenty-five-dollar fine wasn't paid. The criminalization of Black expression in public was a far more serious threat. Insulting a white person was a charge for which free Black women were disproportionately arrested, and the same crime for which Jones had been convicted in New York—larceny, accused by a white man—was a common reason free Black women ended up on trial. Being familiar with all of this, Jones probably worked to make ends meet while she was in town, or to fund her return ticket, avoiding the dangers of the police and clients as she had back home. The local press occasionally published stories about sex workers, generally calling them all "Mary," differentiated only by their hometown. References to "New York Marys" were plentiful.[53]

Why Jones wanted to visit New Orleans is impossible to say for sure. Perhaps she had ties to people there, or perhaps her family roots—however she defined them—lay in the direction of the Caribbean. Likely she was drawn by the city's preeminent free Black culture, a magnet for anyone leveraging the fungibility of Black gender into mobility. The city's tradition of Mardi Gras, which celebrated masquerading and cross-dressing, perhaps meant something to a Black trans woman. Arrests for cross-dressing, as elsewhere in the country, weren't common until decades later, in the 1850s.[54] By then, after the passage of the Fugitive Slave Act and the rising tide of white supremacist violence gripping the country, Jones might have felt it was better to stay close to home. She was also nearing her fifties—a period when the archival record of her life goes dark. Newspaper items from New York in the 1840s offered the occasional, disparagingly written update, mostly to report that she had been arrested for vagrancy. When other cross-dressed people were arrested, they were often compared to her. Jones had truly become a New York idiom.

What mattered to her during those years, or how her life changed, is drowned out by pervasive criminalization. But one exception is worth dwelling on. In its "City Intelligence" column in December of 1844, the *Herald* ran a short item with a long title: "Singular Case—An Oath of Allegiance between Two Noted Characters—Love Correspondence, &c."

"It will be recollected, that some years ago, a negro named Pete Sewally was arrested on a charge of vagrancy, in parading the streets in female attire, enticing men and boys into alleys, and practicing the most revolting offences and, when opportunity favored, robbing his victims," began the column. "His practices were of such a terrible revolting and peculiar character, that the *sobriquet* of Beefsteak Pete was applied to him." Now, a few nights prior, "a genteel looking fellow named John Williams, *alias* Lyness, who has not stuck very rigidly to the paths of honesty was arrested for stealing some packages for Moffat's Life Pills, worth $1, and in his company the notorious Beefsteak Pete was also found." The paper reported that Lyness was indicted for larceny, while Jones was sentenced to yet another six-month prison term "as a vagrant."

But the arrests were only the setup for what struck the *Herald* as newsworthy. "On searching Peter, the following singular document was found," which read:

> I Joseph Liness Do Hereby certify that I have taken an oath in the presences of Theodore Augustus Jackson that I will be a friend to Peter Sewalry till Death Separates us. He giving me the privilege to marry the girl of my choice provided She is beyond a doubt virtuous. I also Swear to tell him everything of the least moment that transpires concerning either of us through Life and I do this voluntarily Swear before God and man.

The oath was signed "Joseph Liness, oct 3rd 1844."

The column provides no commentary but ends with a letter found on Jones. The letter is dated June 11, 1843, and the *Herald* suggests it is written by Lyness, to Jones.

> I take this opportunity to inform you that I am in tolerable health at present hoping that this letter may find you enjoying the same blessing. I arrived home on friday evening found the family in good health except little Angeline she was buried last month we should be plezed to have you come within the space of two or three weeks; otherwise not forget to write
>
> > We pick winter green for pass time
> > if you dont know what they be You can come & see
> > Direct your leter to Olive, Post office
> > > Ulster county, New York.[55]

These two reprinted documents raise yet more possibilities for speculation but offer no definitive answers. Did Jones build a long-term relationship with Lyness? And if legal marriage was impossible because she was trans, not to mention notorious, did the oath stand in as a declaration of their obligations to one another? Did her understanding of it draw on the custom of plaçage she might have witnessed in New Orleans? And was a relationship with a white man governed by economic necessity, love, or some combination of both?

The letter from Lyness to Jones is even more curious. Perhaps he lived in Ulster County with the soon-to-be wife to which his later oath obliged him. And perhaps Jones would sometimes visit him upstate. Maybe she even lived there for some time. The 1850 census records almost 1,600 free Black people as county residents, mostly concentrated in towns like Kingston, Marlborough, New Paltz, and Saugerties. Olive, the city whose post office Lyness named, recorded only thirty-four.[56] Perhaps Jones visited Lyness as part of trips to abolitionist communities in the Hudson Valley.[57] Then again, perhaps repeated trips upstate for prison sentences gave her the same occasion. Or perhaps none of it was true. The *Herald* might have embellished to the point of distortion, or even fabricated the story for readers used to periodic updates. It wouldn't have been the first time that the press had invented a life for Mary Jones.

Speculation is the genre attached to Mary Jones, but not all speculations yield the same return. The penny press was given to libelous speculation about her character as a free Black woman, never passing up the opportunity to exaggerate the duplicity pasted onto her public image. Jones herself made a series of gambles, daring to lean into the "fugitive moments in the hollow of fungibility's embrace," as Snorton puts it.[58] The intense contradictions of the antebellum United States made sex work a trans route to its own sort of speculation: that the contradictions between racial slavery and capitalist wage labor could return just enough to live on, at least sometimes. Still, working with contradiction meant constantly risking outcomes the exact opposite of what she hoped for. The same fungibility attached to Black gender that let her follow the routes of cotton and capital between New York to New Orleans, or negotiate a relationship with John Lyness, was what criminalized her life in a way that resonates for many Black trans women to this day, restricting the possibility of ever living comfortably when the police are lurking around every corner.

The reason why trans women like Mary Jones have historically done sex work is simple: it's a job that embraces contradiction, instead of moralizing work and value. It wasn't that she had no other choice, or no choice at all. Sex work didn't replace "real" work, either. Jones did domestic work, and she sold sex because the service economy arose in this era as the informal sibling to industrial capitalism and slavery. For centuries, around the world, there had been as many ways to live something approximating trans-feminine lives as there were human cultures. Many built that trans femininity directly into kinship, the household, or imbued upon it spiritual and political meaning, so that it didn't stand apart from a normal life. Their multitude of rules and forms had little or nothing to do with European or American customs. But by the early nineteenth century, the global reach of European and American slavery and colonialism had stolen so many bodies, and severed so many people's relationships to land, that the urban, lumpenproletarian model of trans womanhood began to replace all others. Increasingly, trans womanhood was a common strategy that leveraged the mobility of gender and race in the wake of dispossession into something livable. Sex work was its most practical and ubiquitous route. If Jones had been born a generation or two earlier, and had lived life enslaved, her womanhood would have been radically constricted by its constant, immediate ungendering—and perhaps untraceable to historians. If she had been born even earlier, in the place her ancestors called home, she might have lived a life entirely outside of the Western framework of gender. But she lived in the antebellum city, and her life—along with those of Mary Ann Waters, Sally Binns, Lavinia Edwards, and their contemporaries —testifies to how tightly trans womanhood tracks with historical changes in state power and political economy. Like the hijras in British India from chapter 1, Jones is part of the story of how Euro-American forces trans-femininized people around the world without any regard for who they might have otherwise been, pushing them into similar lines of work out of which something resembling trans womanhood emerged as a play for mobility.

It may be surprising that such a recognizably modern trans story can be found two centuries ago, since the downward mobility of becoming a woman, not to mention the criminalization of the racialized and sexualized body, remains to this day a unique drag on trans women's lives in the US if they are Black, Brown, or Indigenous. Two centuries ago, many of the people who embraced trans womanhood might have done so without consciously framing their decisions as a transition from one gender to another. For those who were trans-femininized by the state, the trajectory of their lives was conditioned by the massive liquidation of the countless cultural, linguistic, religious, and kinship idioms that had previously governed their ways of life. Jones was an early example of what could come in the aftermath of such violent upheaval. In the wake of slavery, there was no home, cultural or literal, to return to.[59] She lived by crossing certain gender and color lines, exploiting their many contradictions as much as they criminalized her in return. And for it, she earned a sacred place in a long tradition of Black speculation.

Still, the sober, careful labors of a historian are embarrassingly inadequate before the inventiveness of her life. *Salacia* (2020), a short film by the artist Tourmaline, does what the historical record will never be capable of doing: show us Mary Jones living out the words she spoke at her trial. The film tempers the dizzying mobility of her life by locating her in Seneca Village, a free community where some Black New Yorkers were able to own property before it was destroyed to make way for Central Park. It's unlikely Jones ever lived there, but the decision to imagine her there is brilliant. She is embraced by scenes of Black domesticity and love. Jones sips tea with other women in their finery, at home and smiling in a social world based in belonging. She does sex work, but on the outskirts of the Village, rolling her eyes in boredom just as a white male client (perhaps Robert Haslem) comes. These choices reframe her subsequent movement at nightfall, giving her a backstory history never will. As she walks out of Seneca Village, she encounters a wanted poster adapted from the "Man Monster" lithograph. Jones rips it down from a pole and is crouched over it, ready to cast an Afro-diasporic spell, when she is apprehended by a white police officer.

The film cuts to her in jail, languishing on the floor alone, but her captivity remains the portal to something bigger. An eerie call begins to reverberate in the water of a puddle in her cell. A voice calls out her name: "Mary. Mary!" The film time shifts to archival footage of Sylvia Rivera, holding court on the West Side Piers in Manhattan, over a century and a half later, in the 1990s. Rivera shares that when she "meditates" on the water, she can't help but say, "You gotta keep fighting girly 'cause it's not time for you to cross the River Jordan." That River Jordan, the Hudson, links New York City by water to the Middle Passage, but also across time, back to 1836. The long life of *Mary* as a name for notorious women and queens allows the archival footage to address Jones directly. Rivera reaches back through the tissue of New York and tells Mary to keep fighting.

Moved by the message, Jones pulls the wanted poster out from her clothes and places it on the jail's dirt floor, determined to carry out a difficult spell under the moonlight that fills up the scene. The other jailed Black people in a cell nearby cry out to her, "Take us with you!" to which Jones replies, "This isn't for the faint of heart, darlin'." The spell works, freeing her, and she flees back to Seneca village.

Salacia's aesthetic is deeply saturated by dark blues and a striking dampness, particularly in the jail scene, intensified by shots of the ocean and river. Water truly is the medium through which flows not just space and time but the promise of Black freedom and trans freedom that depends on their distortion.

Among Tourmaline's signal accomplishments is reversing the conventional flow of time through the medium of water. As the third chapter of this book will argue, Black trans women are often politically idealized by those who don't know them. Instead of attending to their circumstances or labors, onlookers claim them as utopian in their manifest suffering in order to certify the goodness of queer and trans politics or community. When it comes to history, Black trans women are often claimed uncomfortably like possessions by those looking backward for guidance, though they do not share in their struggle. In

Salacia, Rivera returns to the antebellum era for the inverse purpose: to help Jones, not to be helped by her. The forward march of trans history sputters out for something far grander in a goosebump-raising moment, as we listen to Rivera call out to Mary. It couldn't be intentional, and yet it somehow feels as though that was exactly who she was calling that day in the 1990s. Rivera asks Jones not to cross the River Jordan just yet. She asks her fellow New Yorker to stay in the struggle, to keep fighting for what is here on this earth—what in this world needs fixing. The bridge between them is not a common identity, a fabulated sisterhood based on a transgender umbrella; it is, rather, a shared struggle on the island of Manhattan, a struggle based in the material stakes of poverty, policing, and sex work.

Like Arthur Jafa's photographic portraits reimagining Jones as defiant and unafraid, Tourmaline does not wish away what *is* known about Jones on the basis of its inflection with anti-Blackness. The film confronts Jones's sex work and imprisonment, but it restores spiritual context and a keen solidarity between trans and free Black New Yorkers alike. In the project of Black speculation, Mary Jones's story is not over. Its ending may never be written, precisely like the looping video that restarts *Salacia* in its installation at New York's Museum of Modern Art every six minutes. The story can't end, because it isn't over. This is not because some "we," in the present, hasn't learned the right lesson from the past, but because trans womanhood weaves stories out of the radical inadequacy of the world that are too alive with contradiction for a simple beginning, middle, and end.

3

Queens of the Gay World

In the faded, sunstroked Los Angeles of the late 1950s, a lone wolf appears on the horizon of Pershing Square. Located in the city's notorious downtown vice district, this small public park is abuzz with the thick atmosphere of a setting June sun. As the man surveys the square city block before him, he inventories the ensemble cast gathered for their daily sundown rituals. In one corner, a Black woman is sweating in wooly taupe, preaching to exhaustion of sin and repentance. Within earshot of her, a clutch of street kids snicker and banter in grubby clothes, chewing on the ends of long finished smokes. A few stray commuters late for their streetcars trot through the square, eyes locked forward. On the opposite end of the park is a small makeshift shed, on the side of which two policemen lean lazily, but watchfully. Despite the flurry of activity, the soundscape of Pershing Square is muted, if not dusky. Only to the trained eye of the solitary man now perched on the street corner is the subterranean life of the park detectable. Slim, wiry figures are camping out here and there, so casual in their tableaux as to look effortless, propped up against benches, water fountains, and bushes. They could be waiting for a bus or for a friend, suspicious only in their perfect innocence. Around them forms a ring, though at a noticeable distance, of much older figures, all men. Dressed more conventionally, as if they had just left the office, they are caught in the paradox of looking so generically normal that they are out of place. They have come here to seek out someone like the lone wolf. They have come to find a youngman in Pershing Square.

Youngman is the novelist John Rechy's term of endearment for the masses of male hustlers that populate the vast American "city of night" of his eponymous 1963 novel.[1] Stretching from Times Square on the East Coast, to New Orleans on the Gulf, to Pershing Square in the Californian West, Rechy's writing offers an unflinching portrait of the sexual underground before the Stonewall riots. *City of Night* is loosely autobiographical, following a Chicano youngman from the borderlands of El Paso and Ciudad Juárez who leaves his mother behind for the relentless, solitary life of a hustler. As an emblem of what the midcentury gay world called "trade," the protagonist isn't queer as the novel's characters understand it. Like countless other young, fit, and anonymous men and boys who filled cities like LA after World War II, his sexuality is economic, not an identity. He has sex with men exclusively for money, looking down on the queers in search of unpaid dates, relationships, and happily ever after. He's a drifter, moving from city to city with a beatnik wanderlust straight out of Kerouac. He has an irrepressible need to seek something he thinks he will never find: the balm for a lonely spirit in a soulless America. He arrives in LA and to Pershing Square anonymous, without a place to live. He has no plan other than doing what he knows best, which is to hustle.

This youngman is the famed gay outlaw. Long before the era of gay marriage and corporate Pride parades, the smoldering cities of postwar America generated the solo gay man as a kind of fugitive. Always on the run from the cops, the gay outlaw had nowhere to rest in the era of white-picket suburbs, *Leave It to Beaver*, and meaningless office jobs in skyscrapers. The gay outlaw took his expulsion from normal society as a badge of honor. He was framed by a conservative public as a menace, a would-be sexual predator, and a dangerous street criminal. In the heavily policed era before Stonewall, he was also the symbol of cool dissent. Leaving behind the stultifying world of 1950s conventionality, he may have been only as free as the change in his pocket from his most recent score, but his destiny was his own. If he could avoid the police, and if he could avoid the truth of his deep loneliness, he answered to no one.

The gay outlaw has long been a romantic fantasy in American queer culture and historical memory.[2] What could be more antisocial than to be a hustler, giving up family, regular work, and normal society for an illegal life lived out in public parks, vice bars, and after-hours joints? What could be further from the idea of gay community than an economy of cheap sex work and cheaper drugs? In the closeted, Cold War era of McCarthyism, weren't gay outlaws the ultimate self-made men, bravely choosing themselves over the death sentence of conformity? That version of the story holds a certain appeal, but it's not actually the story of this youngman. His fate is not so solitary. And his life world, the gay world of LA, is not exactly an antisocial collection of wayward souls. Not long after *City of Night*'s protagonist arrives in Pershing Square, he is swept up by the arrival of the park's *grand dame*, a queen named Miss Destiny. Rechy paints a wild portrait of Destiny. She is a composite figure made of half truths and spectacular lies, but Rechy based her on a real queen he knew, who went on to grace the cover of *ONE Magazine* in 1964, after the publication of the novel.[3]

As a character in Rechy's novel, Destiny is a kaleidoscopic myth, much larger than life. One day she lays on a thick Southern accent, and the next she's from Pennsylvania. One day she explains that she got her name, Destiny, from a rich daddy, but in her next breath he was a poor truck driver. She claims nearly every piece of trade in LA as her "ex-husband," but she dreams of settling down and getting married. "A real wedding" is what she wants, "like every young girl should have at least once"—one where she will descend a grand staircase in a Hollywood hills mansion, and where champagne and cake will be served after the ceremony.[4]

Miss Destiny is a street queen, a poor trans woman who gives Pershing Square its life and its authenticity. Like Marsha P. Johnson of Christopher Street on the other end of the country, Miss Destiny is the patron saint of this outpost in the gay underworld. She dazzles the youngmen who have flocked to LA to make it, taking them into her shoddy apartment and teaching them what it takes to live by hustling. But she also shows them how to live larger than their impoverished and policed lives allow on the surface. She is royalty in every sense. As a trans woman she has two bodies—one given to her in the flesh and one aspirational—and she claims to transcend the material world with its tawdry notions of maleness as the opposite of glamorous femininity. But she is also the gay world's lowly symbol, it's stigmatized calling card. Miss Destiny reigns in Pershing Square because it is in her image that the hopes and dreams of everyone around her in *City of Night* will rise and fall. The hot, cramped, and overpeopled streets, dives, and apartments of downtown LA breathe in and out with the rhythm of a queen's exaltation and her inevitable fall from grace.

Queen still bears the traces of this moment as a term of endearment that transcends gender. But the idea that gay people, or the gay world, had queens-as-in-royalty isn't conventional wisdom. *Queen* is usually understood to be a simple metaphor. Gay culture and camp rituals, after all, are not called "fabulous" for no reason, and *queen* is a term that can be applied to nearly anyone who deserves praise. So what does it matter that the original queens of the gay world were, in many cases, trans street queens? Why were poor trans women like Miss Destiny, who blurred the lines between gay men and trans femininity, the reigning figures of the gritty city of night? Today, a trans woman and a gay man are presented as different species, one defined by gender identity, the other by sexual orientation. They are asked to assemble under an acronym, a tense solidarity barely held together by the letters *L-G-B-T*.

The community even has its ritual combat every June, paying homage to how much the first three of those letters owe the last—or how much some would wish they be kept separate. But the revisionist history that sees gay men and trans women as separate groups, a narrative that serves the ends of US identity politics, isn't just historically inaccurate. Terribly, it can't explain what it means to be a queen. A queen is now just a metaphor, a relic of an era now anachronistic, when gay men were perhaps less sure of their distance from trans femininity.

In the continuing battles over the place of poor trans women in the LGBT movement, this is an especially difficult history to wrestle with. Why has the central symbol of gay culture long been trans femininity? What if the trans queens of the gay world were actual queens, sovereign figures meant to lead all sorts of exiles from American culture labeled deviant? If trans women were once the queens of the gay world, what ended their reign? And what does their power in the past say about the present, when trans misogyny is so ubiquitous that there are formal organizations of gay men dedicated to selling out trans women as the real perverts?[5] What does the queen tell us about the deep entanglement of gay men with trans femininity? What does the queen represent that makes them so uncomfortable?

Maybe the answer is a bit camp, a little too gauche for polite gay society. Perhaps it's an outrageous comparison to liken gay men to trans women, or poor street queens to royalty. But there are clues to this story, the story of Miss Destiny's namesake, hidden in plain sight everywhere in the record of the gay world from the midcentury.

In the mid-1960s, a graduate student in anthropology at the University of Chicago got permission to research an extremely unconventional topic for her dissertation: drag queens. Esther Newton was used to taking risks. As a woman, she was already treated as inferior by the all-male anthropology faculty, who at one point singled out the slacks she wore to campus as unprofessional. One of her advisors told her that "it was important to be attractive and feminine" in her choice of clothes.[6] Newton quickly had to learn in this environment to closet her burgeoning lesbian identity. Studying "homosexuality" for her PhD was quite a gamble considering she hoped to maintain a professional cover as straight and land a career as a professor. Whether or not she was drawn to studying gay men because she was a lesbian is impossible to tell from the carefully tailored prose of her published research. But in her memoir, *My Butch Career*, Newton shares that it was during her lonely early days as a graduate student that the idea of studying drag queens was planted in her mind. Cal, a fellow student in her department, had asked her out. Sitting on Newton's couch sipping drinks after dinner, he confessed that he was gay. He had clearly clocked Esther as a fellow traveler. "Freed by my own drinks, I answered that I thought I was, too," Newton remembers.[7] It was a moment that would change the course of her life. Cal introduced her to the Chicago gay scene later that summer. Although she had originally planned to do fieldwork somewhere overseas, watching the drag queen Skip Arnold perform for the first time in 1965 made such a powerful impression that she decided to write a term paper about the Chicago drag scene. Skip became her first informant. From there, her eventual PhD project took root.[8]

Even if Newton passed to her colleagues as a straight outsider studying gay people, her research was highly unconventional. In the 1960s it was rare for anthropologists to study American culture at all; anthropology had since its birth been a discipline in which Westerners departed for fieldwork far from home, pretending that non-Western cultures were "primitive" and easy to objectify. While American anthropologists had used those ethnocentric and racist principles in their extensive studies of Indigenous cultures in North America, for Newton to do fieldwork in urban gay bars throughout the Midwest was a bit renegade. So was the premise of her eventual study, *Mother*

Camp: Female Impersonators in America: that gay people had their own culture. In her memoir, Newton explains the premise "that gays were not just a category of sick isolates but a group, and so had a culture, was a breathtaking leap whose daring is hard to recapture now, when the term 'gay community' is so familiar."[9] She used her position as an anthropologist to argue, against the grain, that gay people were on the whole culturally similar to the rest of America, rather than strange exceptions. This was a stunning claim when homosexuality was still illegal in most states, as was cross-dressing in many cities. The cover of the anthropologist, the would-be outsider, had worked spectacularly. Newton retained her closeted pretense in academia—a front that allowed her innovative work to be taken seriously. Nearly everyone she met in the drag bars of the Midwest, on the other hand, assumed correctly that she was a lesbian, granting her intimate access to their lives.

Mother Camp is a study of professional "female impersonators"—drag queens, like the ones who still perform at bars today. By grounding her anthropological analysis of drag as a type of job, Newton painted an uncommonly detailed portrait of "the gay world" in the 1960s through the lens of class. What she saw was a kind of underworld. A wide variety of people from all walks of life affected by the stigma of homosexuality were forced to gather furtively, under constant threat of police raids. As a result, unlike the rest of American society, the gay world was quite diverse in class. At bars on the North Side of Chicago, Newton found that bankers rubbed elbows with construction workers. Businessmen and middle management drank alongside waiters, hairdressers, and actors. They were all exiled from normal society because they were gay. Although white men predominated, she found that lesbians weren't scarce, and that gay bars in white neighborhoods were far less racially segregated than most straight establishments. Yet even though the stigma attached to being "deviant" exiled everyone to the bars, Newton noticed that there was still a strict hierarchy inside the gay world. In fact, the gay version of class largely reinvented straight society's emphasis on professional prestige. This is where drag queens came into the picture. The drag queen, Newton observed, was the central symbol of being gay—for everyone. The drag queen symbolized the social situation of midcentury gay people. She was the purest incarnation of the stigma attached to effeminacy—that which threatened to reveal and discredit gay people in straight society. While many tried to closet themselves to avoid that stigma, acting straight in their work lives and only "letting their hair down" in gay bars or at home, drag queens embraced effeminacy. Unlike everyone else, drag queens made a career out of being gay. For that reason, drag queens were revered, performing in defiance of a collectively shared stigma on stage.[10]

Yet Newton also observed a major class division in 1960s drag, around which *Mother Camp* is structured. The professional female impersonator was strictly in drag onstage. When her gig was over, she would slip back into men's clothes and wipe off her makeup. She would almost never leave the bar cross-dressed—which was illegal in many places. Drag queens, in other words, were performers. Almost all of them, at least publicly, considered themselves men doing a job. They were not trying to be women by dressing in drag; they were merely performing. And by regarding themselves as professional performers—if poorly paid and highly exploited ones—they appealed to the class status that professionalism conferred on them in the gay world. Despite embracing the stigma of effeminacy, they carefully managed and monetized it, turning femininity into a job. Professional drag queens were admired precisely because they were professionals. Newton wagered that they were, in fact, the most highly valued icons of the gay world—more admired than even masculine gay men who passed for straight. Drag queens onstage were the only ones who could make fun of or criticize straight people and get away with it. Their biting wit had the built-in insurance policy of being part of an act.[11]

In contrast with professional drag queens, who were only playing at being women onstage, Newton learned that the very bottom of the gay social hierarchy was the province of street queens. In almost total contrast to professional queens, street queens were "the underclass of the gay world."[12] Although they embraced effeminacy, too, they did so in the wrong place and for the wrong reason: in public and outside of professional work. As a result, Newton explained, the street queens "are never off stage … Their way of life is collective, illegal, and immediate." Because they didn't get paid to be feminine and were locked out of even the most menial of nightlife jobs, Newton observed that their lives were perceived to revolve around "confrontation, prostitution, and drug 'highs.'"[13] Even in a gay underworld where everyone was marked as deviant, it was the sincere street queens who tried to live as women who were punished most for what was celebrated—and paid—as an act onstage. When stage queens lost their jobs, they were often socially excluded like trans women. Newton explained that when she returned to Kansas City one night during her fieldwork, she learned that two poor queens she had met had recently lost their jobs as impersonators. Since then, they had become "indistinguishable from street fairies," growing out their hair long and wearing makeup in public—even "'passing' as girls in certain situations," in addition to earning a reputation for taking pills.[14] They were now treated harshly by everyone in the local scene. Most people wouldn't even speak to them in public. Professional drag queens who didn't live as women still had to avoid being seen as too "transy" in their style and demeanor. One professional queen that Newton interviewed explained why: it was dangerous to be transy because it reinforced the stigma of effeminacy without the safety of being onstage. "I think what you do in your bed is your business," he told Newton, echoing a middle-class understanding of gay privacy, "[but] what you do on the street is everybody's business."[15]

The first street queen who appears in *Mother Camp* is named Lola, a young Black trans girl who is "'becoming a woman,' as they say."[16] Newton met Lola at her dingy Kansas City apartment, where she lived with Tiger, a young gay man, and Godiva, a somewhat more respectable queen. What made Godiva more respectable than Lola wasn't just a lack of hormonal transition. It was that Godiva could work as a female impersonator because she wasn't trying to sincerely live as a woman. Lola, on the other hand, was permanently out of work because being Black and trans made her unhireable, including in female impersonation. When Newton entered their apartment, which had virtually no furniture, she found Lola lying on "a rumpled-up mattress on the floor" and entertaining three "very rough-looking young men." These kinds of apartments, wrote Newton, "are not 'homes.' They are places to come in off the street."[17] The extremely poor trans women who lived as street queens, like Lola, "literally live outside the law," Newton explained. Violence and assault were their everyday experiences, drugs were omnipresent, and sex work was about the only work they could do. Even if they didn't have "homes," street queens "do live in the *police* system."[18]

As a result of being policed and ostracized by their own gay peers, Newton felt that street queens were "dedicated to 'staying out of it'" as a way of life. "From their perspective, all of respectable society seems square, distant, and hypocritical. From their 'place' at the very bottom of the moral and status structure, they are in a strategic position to experience the numerous discrepancies between the ideals of American culture and the realities."[19] Yet, however withdrawn or strung out they were perceived to be, the street queens were hardly afraid to act. On the contrary, they were regarded by many as the bravest and most combative in the gay world. In the summer of 1966, street queens in San Francisco fought back at Compton's Cafeteria, an all-night venue popular with sex workers and other poor gay people. After management had called the police on a table that was hanging out for hours ordering nothing but coffee, an officer grabbed the arm of one street queen. As the historian Susan Stryker recounts, that queen threw her coffee in the police officer's face, "and a melee erupted." As the queens led the patrons in throwing everything on their tables at the cops—who called for backup—a full-blown riot erupted onto the street. The queens beat the police with their purses "and kicked them with their high-heeled shoes."[20] A similar incident was documented in 1959, when drag queens fought back against the police at Cooper's Donuts in Los Angeles by throwing donuts—and punches.[21] How many more, unrecorded, times street queens fought back is anyone's guess. The most famous event came in 1969, when street queens led the Stonewall rebellion in New York City. Newton shares in *Mother Camp* that she wasn't surprised to learn it was the street queens who carried Stonewall. "Street fairies," she wrote, "having nothing to lose."[22]

Clearly most other people in the gay world thought they did have something to lose in standing up to the straight world and its police. And they were increasingly willing to turn their backs on street queens in self-interest. When the second edition of *Mother Camp* was published in 1979, Newton included a new preface reflecting on what had changed since Stonewall. In about ten years, the status of the queen had shifted dramatically in her eyes. If drag queens had been "gay male culture 'heroes' in the mid-sixties," the 1970s had seen a profound shift toward a masculine style. Muscles, moustaches, and leather were the new calling cards of gay men. And the pride movement that had formed in the wake of Stonewall, which demanded people come out of the closet and proclaim a public identity, had revolutionized the way that gay culture managed stigma. No longer were the queens seen as the symbols of defiant stigma at the heart of gay life. By being out, proud, and masculine, gay men were accruing unprecedented political and cultural visibility in the 1970s. This new experience incentivized them to separate themselves from the queens of the prior decade. "In the last ten years there has been an enormous struggle within the gay male community to come to terms with the stigma of effeminacy," wrote Newton.[23] Many gay men no longer wanted to be associated with effeminacy or trans femininity at all. In 1973, activists had succeeded in having homosexuality removed from the *Diagnostic and Statistical Manual*. Being gay was no longer considered a mental illness.[24] Suddenly, homosexuality might be called normal, or even healthy—words that would have been nearly unthinkable in the early 1960s. Cross-dressing and taking hormones didn't fit into this new version of gay men *as men*, their ticket to being respected in American society.

Trans femininity, in short, didn't seem to have a place in the gay world of the 1970s. Newton felt this was a change correlate to maleness, whiteness, and wealth, guessing that "Black and Hispanic gays (and poor whites) have retained the effeminate drag style."[25] But trans women had a new white and middle-class ideal in the '70s, too: the transsexual. This new kind of trans woman wouldn't just take hormones but could surgically change sex to pass in her own right, disappearing into American society much like gay men hoped to—at least, that was the way it was sold in the media. Newton mused that "the transsexual phenomenon" might be a kind of counterpart to the new masculine norm in gay men's culture: "If you don't like being a man, get out. America: Love it or leave it."[26]

The problem was, though, that street queens weren't transsexuals: they were far too poor to transition like that. Now pushed out of the mainstream gay movement, they didn't have the wealth it took to get a transsexual diagnosis in the 1970s. The new medical model explicitly kept out poor girls who didn't pass well, who did sex work, or who couldn't promise to live a middle-class, heterosexual life after surgery. Most Black and Brown queens didn't even bother with the clinics selling high-priced surgeries and hormone therapies.[27] Newton felt that queens in general were being broadly discarded in the 1970s from their once-exalted place in the gay world. But street queens were the ones who by far suffered the most. They increasingly became unwanted, especially by gay men, who rejected the notion that they had anything in common with trans femininity.

This is the moment when the story of Pride usually begins: in New York City in the early 1970s, with Sylvia Rivera, Marsha P. Johnson, and the trans women of color who had helped found the gay liberation movement after the Stonewall riots. Within only a few years they found themselves kicked out of that same movement by gay and lesbian leaders who wanted, above all, to be welcomed as normal men and women, distant from the stigma trans femininity embodied. But this version of the story still isn't quite right. If Sylvia and Marsha's role is contextualized in the tectonic shifts from the 1960s to the '70s that Newton observed, there is a glaring point that is rarely taken into consideration: Sylvia and Marsha weren't generic trans women. They did not call themselves "transgender women of color," as they are often described today. They were street queens, and their exclusion from gay politics is the story of the street queen's reign coming to a violent end.

In the wake of Stonewall, gay liberation activism exploded in New York. Sylvia Rivera got involved in the Gay Activists Alliance at New York University in 1970. From the very beginning, some of the gay and lesbian membership of the GAA didn't want her and the street queens involved. They charged that she was "copying and flaunting some of the worse aspects of female oppression" by living as a transvestite and drag queen.[28] After the GAA organized a ball in June 1970 to commemorate the Stonewall rebellion, the NYU administration banned them from holding future dances.

In response, Rivera and Marsha P. Johnson led the GAA's five-day-long occupation of Weinstein Hall. When a protest ball was scheduled in September, the New York Police Department showed up to clear out the occupiers. As soon as the cops appeared, most of the non-trans protestors—largely college-student gay activists—left, abandoning Rivera, Johnson, and the queens to an NYPD that relished targeting them. The queens considered the desertion to be nothing short of a betrayal. They wrote a collective statement, "Street Transvestites for Gay Power," which they delivered to the GAA leadership. In it, they didn't reject the liberatory politics of gay power or propose that gay and trans politics should go their separate ways. Instead, they made clear that the difference brewing was political. "IF you want Gay Liberation," they wrote, "then you're going to have to fight for it." As the queens saw it, after Weinstein Hall "the question is, do we want Gay Power or Pig Power?" The non-trans gay activists, many of whom were NYU students expecting a life of upward mobility from their college degree, were not willing to risk open confrontation with the police. The street queens saw this as an abandonment of gay power that endorsed police violence. They adopted a political position informed by the total criminalization of their lives. "Once you start you're not going to be able to stop because if you do you'll lose everything," they wrote to the GAA. "So if you want to fight for your rights, then fight till the end."[29]

This first betrayal led Rivera and Johnson to found Street Transvestite Action Revolutionaries (STAR) shortly thereafter. The motivation for this landmark trans liberation group was not a split over identity—between gay and trans interests. Rather, as the Weinstein Hall incident reveals, their organizing expressed a political difference rooted in class. Street queens' understanding of gay liberation was more radical and concrete than that of the general membership of the GAA. Their militant stance was rooted in the experience of living at the bottom of the social hierarchy, including in the gay world. Young, homeless, and targeted by constant violence, the street queens of New York City were poorer, Blacker, and Browner than the rest of the gay liberation crowd, which made living as women exceptionally difficult. Rivera's life story was typical of the street queens who banded together in STAR. Born on Long Island to a Puerto Rican and Venezuelan family, by the time she was in the fourth grade she started wearing makeup to school. She had also learned that older boys and men had a sexual interest in girls like her. By the time she was ten, she was doing street sex work to help support her family, headed by her grandmother, whom she called Viejita. "My grandmother used to come home," Rivera remembered, "and it smelled like a French whorehouse, but that didn't stop me."[30] Still, the neighbors admonished Viejita that her grandchild was nothing more than a cheap *pato* in their eyes. Worrying about the effect on her grandmother, Rivera decided to leave home for the city around age ten or eleven. She arrived at Times Square, a notorious vice neighborhood, to find a community of poor sex workers awaiting her. The street queens who worked Forty-Second Street would become her new family. And it was there that she met Marsha P. Johnson, who was a teenager at the time. Part of a tight-knit community of queens, they hustled and avoided the police as best they could.

Rivera and Johnson are often celebrated today as trans women of color, as if that were a clear-cut category that was different from gay men. However, neither of them made that sort of distinction at the time. In an interview recorded at the end of 1970, both use a range of different words to describe themselves, including *gay*, *drag queen*, and *transvestite*.[31] Indeed, for many street queens, the philosophical difference between being gay and trans was irrelevant. As noted above, they were too poor to afford medical transition; they also likely would have been turned away from any of the doctors prescribing hormones in New York. More importantly, the concrete conditions of their lives weren't organized around a difference between gender and sexuality. Cross-dressing was illegal, and so was sex work—and both were based entirely on public perception. The police didn't much care whether someone identified as a woman or a gay man; in jail, they would be treated horrifically either way. As such, it didn't much matter how they felt on the inside, or what words they used to describe themselves. When they came to organizing under the banner of STAR, Rivera and Johnson saw themselves as true adherents to the gay liberation movement, rather than a separatist trans movement. They had a political consciousness born of the 1960s, the era that Newton documented in *Mother Camp*. And like Newton, they analyzed their lives in class terms. In the 1970 interview, Rivera explained that "it's not just transvestites who call me Sylvia or who consider or treat me as a she. This is how people respect you. This is respect." Her experience of marginalization and oppression gave her insight into "the bourgeois society" that expected "a transvestite or a woman" to "do all the washing or all the cooking" in relationships with men. "That's a lot of baloney," she said. "Men are oppressive. They just oppress you in all different ways."[32] Fighting the oppression of men and the institutions that maintained their hegemony, like the police, was something Rivera understood to ideally unite street queens with feminists and gay activists, not separate them.

However, STAR's radical political vision proved immensely unpopular with a newly masculine gay movement and the growing anti-trans tenor of some lesbian feminists.[33] The unresolved tensions of Weinstein Hall came to a dramatic head in 1973 at Christopher Street Liberation Day, the annual commemoration of Stonewall today called Pride. Rivera had been scheduled to speak on the stage set up in Washington Square Park in Greenwich Village, where the march ended. But when she arrived, she found a contingent of gay people who were staunchly against street queens and tried to stop her from speaking. Rivera had to physically fight her way up to the stage, after which she delivered a legendary speech commemorated by its first line, "Y'all better quiet down."

The context in which Rivera delivered that opening line is

preserved in video footage that has recirculated since the artist and activist Tourmaline freed it from archival obscurity and digitized it.[34] The shaky camera swerves from within the crowd, pointed up at the stage. The occasional phrase spoken into a microphone is nearly drowned out by a soundtrack of constant disagreement: yelling, cheering, booing, and a hundred conversations raging in every direction. The tension in the air is palpable even in grainy black and white.

A lesbian first took the microphone and addressed the rowdy crowd. "All right, it's up to the gay people, whadd'ya wanna do?" she asked about Rivera. A gay man then took the mic and added: "Listen, we don't know what you want." He polled the crowd to see if they wanted her to speak. "Will the people who want it say yes," he directed—to which the crowd roared back in approval. "That's the end of the conversation," he declared.

As Rivera was finally ushered onstage, a muffled voice can be heard screaming off screen, perhaps saying, "They're going to take over," in reference to the queens. But the organizer holding the mic quieted the interrupter, emphasizing that "she is speaking." Rivera then burst onto the stage and delivered her first line in a jumpsuit pictured in many photos from the day. While the crowd had cheered when they first saw her, a chorus of boos followed. Leaning one hand on the microphone stand and holding her hip with the other, Rivera looked out on the crowd in disappointment, like a mother chastising her children. After watching them for a few seconds and conferring with an organizer onstage, she whisked the microphone up to her mouth and lobbed her first line to the park to behave themselves. Another voice, somehow just as loud without a microphone, shot back at her, brimming with venom: "Shut the fuck up!"

Walking casually across the stage as if to prove she was unafraid, Rivera screamed her speech out in angry bursts, stopping every so often to wait out the battery of insults, boos, and jeers returned to her. She delivered a powerful indictment of the blatant trans misogyny of the gay liberation movement that had distracted from the political cause she was there to speak about: "your gay brothers and sisters in jail!" While Christopher Street Liberation Day had increasingly commemorated the Stonewall rebellion through the new gender-normative style of the moment, the most criminalized in the community who couldn't live up to that norm were left behind or unwelcome. Rivera reminded the crowd that incarcerated gay and trans people wrote a steady stream of letters to her and the members of STAR, asking for help. The prisoners would have asked everyone in gay liberation for help, but "you don't do a goddamn thing for them," she railed.

Like a wedge, trans misogyny had fractured the political solidarity of the gay liberation banner in less than four years. The abandonment of the incarcerated was also the abandonment of street queens, considering they were hit the hardest by police violence and violence from men. "Have you ever been beaten up and raped in jail?" Rivera asked the crowd. "Now think about it." By giving up the anti-police focus of Stonewall, the gay movement was leaving its sisters to rot in jail. "The women have tried to fight for their sex changes or to become women," yelled Rivera. "They write 'STAR'" on their letters instead of "the women's groups. They do not write 'women.' They do not write 'men.' They write 'STAR' because we're trying to do something for them." Failed by both women's liberation and gay liberation, the STAR banner was the only one still directed at patriarchal violence, sexual assault, police brutality, and mass incarceration. This Rivera knew in her bones, her flesh, and her soul.

"I have been to jail," she railed at the crowd. "I have been raped. And beaten. Many times! By men, heterosexual men that do not belong in the homosexual shelter. But, do you do anything for them? No. You tell me to go and hide my tail between my legs."

At this point Rivera was leaning forward with the microphone perched beneath her lips, so that her voice rang out at maximum volume, blanketing the crowd.

"I will not put up with this shit," she warned them. "I have been beaten. I have had my nose broken. I have been thrown in jail. I have lost my job. I have lost my apartment for gay liberation. And you all treat me this way? What the fuck's wrong with you all? Think about that!"

A segment of the crowd applauded these lines before Rivera moved into the final act of her speech. "I believe in the gay power," she boomed, reminding the crowd of their common cause. "I believe in us getting our rights, or else I would not be out there fighting for our rights. That's all I wanted to say to you people." She then urged them not to forget about the gay and trans people in jail, giving them the address of STAR house on East Second Street, where they could rejoin the cause forged at Stonewall. "The people are trying to do something for all of us," roared Rivera. "Not men and women that belong to a white middle class, white club. And that's what you all belong to!"

The crowd resounded as Rivera bellowed, "Revolution now!" and led a chant to spell out "gay power" one letter at a time. By the end, the crowd sounded more unified than when she had first taken the stage. Out of breath from shouting, Rivera gave one last "Gay power!" with every ounce of energy she had, before bowing her head and walking offstage to loud applause.

Rivera's speech wasn't the cause of the split in gay liberation. Rather, it reflected what was by then an overwhelming truth: the gay world and the gay movement did not want street queens in their ranks anymore. If Rivera, like Johnson, had worked in leadership positions and put her life on the line since the Stonewall riots, she was a long way from being crowned queen of gay liberation in Washington Square Park. The political mood of the 1970s reflected the broader social and cultural shift that Newton observed in her second preface to *Mother Camp*. The queen of the gay world had been dethroned.

To call the 1970s the end of the queen's reign may be a camp way to put it, but the point runs deep. What happened in 1973 in New York reverberated through a series of political campaigns in the name of trans misogyny that had been building around the world for over a century. As chapter 1 explained, the global trans panic of the nineteenth century was instigated by a fear of trans-feminine people as a threat to colonial sovereignty. The British administrators in the Northwestern Provinces of India imagined *hijras* to be a kind of shadow dynasty with a king who ruled over a population disloyal to the British Crown. In the United States, federally funded anthropologists recorded in minute detail the political roles that many Two-Spirit people occupied in their home nations. We'wha—a Zuni *lhamana* who in the 1880s spent six months in Washington, DC, meeting the speaker of the House of Representatives and President Cleveland—assumed a range of diplomatic roles in her pueblo. Her political and spiritual work to mediate with colonizers cast her and other Two-Spirit people as threats to settler sovereignty.[35] The policing and attack on street queens in US vice districts became the internal counterpart to this colonial project: to neutralize the sovereignty of the shadow world led by the screaming queens who wouldn't accept being ruled oppressively from without. What happened in Washington Square Park was not unrelated, however distinct and local its causes may have been.

In the 1970s, the US gay and lesbian movement turned on trans femininity. Many gay and lesbian people allied openly with the state to police the streets and rid cities of their queens, uniting longtime enemies. The increasingly gender-normative gay and lesbian movement reasoned that if they sold out the queens, they might be welcomed into a sanitized, middle-class version of citizenship from which they used to be excluded. And they weren't wrong: looking back from the present ubiquity of gay marriage and other privatized civil rights, that is precisely what happened. However, their betrayal has hardly served to extinguish anti-gay movements, and gay rights in the US, built on the right to privacy, are in constant danger of being washed away by courts bought and paid for by conservative interests and violent movements. At the same time, the poorest of trans women live in conditions that have changed remarkably little since the 1970s.

But the fall of the trans queens wasn't just a financial calculation on the part of the gay movement; it was also a spiritual sacrilege. To understand why, a return to Los Angeles and Pershing Square is in order.

John Rechy's chapter in *City of Night* chronicling Miss Destiny might have been titled "The Tragedy of Queen Destiny." Like Shakespeare's original title for "The Tragedie of King Richard the Second," Rechy paints a portrait of a queen who falls from the highest of stations to total ruin, betrayed by her subjects, much like Sylvia Rivera and Marsha P. Johnson in the 1970s. The quiet narrator of *City of Night*, the youngman come to Pershing Square, faithfully chronicles her demise with a tenderness born of the genre of tragedy. He senses the end of her reign coming but is powerless to stop the tides of fate.

Destiny is not just a street queen but sees herself as the literal queen of her gay world. If the word *queen* is more than mere metaphor, Destiny's campy penchant for poorly quoting Shakespeare to the other femmes and youngmen of LA is the first clue. Destiny is a larger-than-life character in *City of Night*, but Rechy was not inventing something in literature that did not exist in the real Los Angeles of his youth. Street queens lived something like literary lives, even in poverty. They practiced an art of living forged in the combination of beautiful trans femininity and material lack. Denied access to the new transsexual technologies for changing sex, the street queen inherited an older lineage of trans femininity. Hers was a spiritual vocation in the magic of transubstantiation: changing one substance into another. This alchemy of sex was how one degraded form of flesh—maleness—might transform into a glamorous, exalted state of high femininity. Street queens were not superficial in their "female impersonation." As the ultimate mimics, the street queen's art of appearances contained a metaphysical promise that the professional drag queens of *Mother Camp* couldn't dream of matching: she would really become a beautiful woman one day. And she wouldn't apologize for what was a magnificent feat, a higher calling. On the contrary, she boldly demanded recognition for it as royalty.

Strangely, for street queens in the midcentury, the problem of becoming a woman created a situation that shared much in common with the monarchs after which they were named. The street queen, like a monarch, had two bodies. One was the earthly body into which she was born as a mortal: male and flawed. The second was a metaphysical body, the promised form of high femininity and womanhood to which she strived. Miss Destiny had received a divine messenger early in childhood to announce the dilemma, a fairy voice and femme conscience named Miss Thing. At a young age, Miss Thing explained what it meant to have two bodies as a comedy of errors. "Why, how ridiculous!—" she reassured the frightened trans child. "That petuh between your legs simpuhlee does not belong, dear."[36] That "petuh" was not an intractable mark of failure, the proof that she could never be a girl. On the contrary, Miss Thing taught Destiny that it was a signal of her fate. She was destined for a higher calling. She would transcend the ridiculous and become a real woman.

The idea that a king or queen had two bodies was the legal foundation of the Tudor-era monarchy in England.[37] Although the king was a human being with a mortal body called the "body natural," he was understood to have also a second body as ruler, his "body politic." This second body was metaphysical and angelic, invisible to be sure, but perhaps the aura of power that accompanied him everywhere. More like a god than human, the king's body politic was not just infallible but immortal. The doctrine of the king's two bodies was a clever concept designed to ensure continuity in a dynasty: when the king died, only his mortal body natural was said to die. His body politic lived on, investing itself in the body of the next person to assume the throne. (This process was literalized again most recently in 2022 when, upon the death of Queen Elizabeth II, King Charles III was an immediate invention. In some invisible process, the body politic of the crown transferred from queen to king, and from female to male.)

In his classic 1950s study of this idea, *The King's Two Bodies*, Ernst Kantorowicz terms this doctrine the "political theology" of sovereignty. The king is not just a political ruler but half divine. And his second body, the divine body politic, was especially strange. In sixteenth-century England, legal commentators claimed that his divine political body quite literally incorporated his subjects into him. In this way, the crown was said to hold the subjects of the king in trust, in his name under the law. But as a theological doctrine, the point was also meant figuratively: the king was united in body with his people. In the "Body politic" of the kingdom, wrote one jurist, "he is the Head, and they," the people, "are the Members."[38] This spiritual and political union between king and people meant that all the mortals of the realm were uplifted into contact with the divine by being ruled. The divinity of the body politic uplifted all mortal bodies, including the king's natural body. Incredibly, the origin of this idea is an older Latin doctrine for deciding the sex of "hermaphrodites." If an individual's sex was in doubt in fourteenth-century Italy, whichever sex appeared to predominate would be recognized by the law. That predominate sex, which was said to rule over the other and thus incorporate it, was then analogized to the political body of the king. As Kantorowicz put it: "What fitted the two sexes of an hermaphrodite, fitted juristically also the two bodies of a king."[39]

Miss Destiny had all these trappings of a queen. In addition to having two bodies, she had to be crowned to confirm her fate, a story she tells the narrator of *City of Night*. Hers was not a literal crown, of course. Instead, to become a woman in the world she had to be given her name, like any monarch in a dynasty. The fated name Destiny was bestowed on her in a kind of farcical coronation by a man named, of all things, Duke. After being kicked out of her home as a teenager, Miss Destiny had hitchhiked to Philadelphia. As soon as she arrived in the city, she bought "a flaming-red dress and high-heeled sequined shoes." Draped in the finery of femininity, she gloried in people taking her to be "real" for the first time. She was finally being treated as a woman. And so, it didn't take long for her to meet a rich daddy at a party. This man, Duke, was fixated on her from across the room. He walked over to her with a singularity of purpose.

The queen explains to the narrator: "Why, he comes to me and says—just like that—'You Are My Destiny!'"

She pauses the story here to explain, "I thought he said, 'You Are *Miss* Destiny,' mistaking me you know for some other girl." Worried that her new paramour might realize she wasn't a real woman if she didn't seize the opportunity, she fired back with barely a second thought: "I am *Miss* Destiny." Only, the Duke seemed to have misheard *her* now, thinking that she had said "I am *his* destiny." But the mistake played out in her favor. When the hostess of the party came over and complimented her beauty, the Duke chimed in to confirm that she was, indeed, *his* destiny.

"And from then on I am Miss Destiny," she explains to the narrator. She was coronated a queen by a Duke in Philadelphia.[40]

The tenuousness of her claim to realness, which originated in a campy miscommunication, dramatizes the dangers of reigning as a street queen. Incorporating two bodies is a high-stakes fate for Miss Destiny, which she quickly learned when Duke abandoned her not long after they fell in love. Subsequently, she returned to street sex work to survive. She tells the young-man listening to her life story that she would always tell johns that she was on her period to avoid being found out. But if she were ever clocked—and she often was—violence was never far behind.[41]

Worse, as the youngman chronicles, the highest of the queens, like Destiny, seem given to the lowest of extravagant depressions. This is because their realness, their feminine sovereignty, is never secure on earth. Like a paranoid ruler expecting betrayal at the hands of someone in her court, so, too, the queen constantly fears being clocked, even in the gay world, and brought back down to earth from her high station to being a mere man in a dress. One night at Destiny's shoddy apartment, as a group of queens entertain a group of rough men, everyone manically taking pills, smoking weed, and downing liquor, Destiny falls apart. Feeling lonely, paranoid, and unadmired by her subjects, she begins to lash out at them. "I! don't! know! what! Iamdoing! here! amongst all this *tuh-rash*!" she screams at her court. 'I! Went! To! College!!! And Read Shakespeare!!!!"[42]

The queen is conscious of the tragic fates of so many Shake-spearean rulers, where the affliction of two bodies can strike at any time, transforming the monarch into a fool. Betrayal is the only constant in Shakespearean tragedy, and Miss Destiny's depression feels like being betrayed by her subjects' lack of devotion. Worst of all, none of the poor youngmen or street queens in her apartment get the reference—except, it turns out, for the narrator, who tells her that he has read Shakespeare. This interrupts Miss Destiny's depression for a moment. Trained by a hard life to be suspicious, she tests him by asking if he knows who Desdemona is, the woman betrayed by con-niving men in *The Tempest*.

He replies yes. He knows Desdemona's tragic tale. And the narrator feels something shift in the air in that moment. "Something was released inside Miss Destiny and something established between us" through the Shakespearean reference. It is a strange something "yearned for with others from person to person in this locked world": the promise of real love. A love that would treat Miss Destiny as a real woman has tormented her in its scarcity her whole life. Without it, she has felt only "the loneliness churning beneath the gay façade desperately awake every moment shouting to be spoken, to be therefore shared." Miss Destiny lives in her mind as a tragic Desdemona, hoping for the love of a man but worried he will betray her, revealing her queen's body to be nothing but a degraded mortal's—a mere man.[43]

"Queens are fooled more often than they admit," observes the narrator solemnly.[44] As powerful as the street queen's promise of turning a man's body into a woman's might be, that brush with the divine is always haunted by the threat of its reversal in a cruel world of trans misogyny. Destiny's depression makes her a tragic figure—one destined, perhaps, to fall into hell instead of ruling the gay world as its queen.

Maybe. But then again, maybe not. The peculiar dilemma of trans womanhood—having two bodies—keeps the story ambiguous. And Miss Destiny wields that ambiguity better than any. She suddenly shifts the scale of her speech. She tells them that sometimes, "when Im very high" and sitting at one of the bars, "I imagine that an angel suddenly appears." This angel has come to signal Judgment Day in the gay world. "And the angel says, 'All right, boys and girls, this is it, the world is ending, and Heaven and Hell will be to spend eternity just as you are now, in the same place among the same people— Forever!'"[45] This, Destiny knows, is a very dangerous gamble, for the gay life has been a miserable one for them all, exiled and discarded as the deviants of America. But the risk of the angel's game is highest for her. If she stays for eternity in Pershing Square, she will never resolve the dilemma of her two bodies. She will never succeed in her quest for transubstantiation. Since a young age, her fate has been to transcend the mortal world, to become angelic herself by becoming a beautiful, real woman. She can't become real if she is forced to live in the limbo of her life as a street queen. Heaven the angel's announcement is not. Though it is a kind of hell, it is perhaps better read as purgatory, where trans misogyny and poverty would rule her existence. Forever.

Knowing this, Destiny tries to run away from the angel. "But I cant run fast enough for the evil angel, he sees me and stops me and Im Caught."[46] The reign of the queen has played out its fate as a Shakespearean tragedy. Because realness isn't really under her sovereignty but belongs to the judgment of an evil world, there will be no escape for Miss Destiny.

Miss Destiny's tragedy is a seductive parable for what really happened to street queens. As Esther Newton observed and Sylvia Rivera and Marsha P. Johnson experienced firsthand, the gay world really did betray its queens in the wake of Stonewall. It was first and foremost a political betrayal, selling out the queens for a new gender normative version of gay. But given the divine importance of the street queen's two bodies, it was also a spiritual betrayal. Miss Destiny's fate was seemingly written in advance, leaving the narrator of *City of Night* to watch on helplessly as the evil angel's prophecy came to pass. He could do no more than offer her the image of Desdemona in solidarity. Yet the better reference would be Shakespeare's *Richard II*, which tells the story of the king falling into the depths of human corruption precisely because he has a man's body attached to his divine body, making him vulnerable to being deposed. Miss Destiny seems to suffer the same fate, replaced by the masculine gay men on the horizon. So, too, for Sylvia and Marsha, kicked out of the gay movement for which they had put their lives on the line.

The problem with tragedy, however, is that it lets the real culprits off the hook by casting the queen's fall from grace as foretold by the fates. The evil angel is a symbol of judgment, but in truth he is merely the mouthpiece for the severe oppression that street queens face, including from their gay subjects. What is holding back Miss Destiny from being real, from being happy and living as a woman, isn't divine judgment; it is the mundane world she lives in. Indeed, 1950s America treats her as unreal and undeserving of anything other than a criminal existence in the underworld. That she has made of that situation a life worthy of the title Queen testifies to her tenacious magic. But, in the end, the street queen cannot transubstantiate without a world that believes in magic. She may know herself to be real, but if no one around her believes it—and if men keep beating her, the police keep arresting her, and the medical establishment keeps hormones out of reach—her exalted femininity won't matter. The art of appearance, the work of the queen, cannot be made real without concrete political struggle. If her gay subjects abandon her to the judgment of a cruel world, even the queen cannot rise above their sin.

Tragedy, that very Christian narrative of the predestined fall from grace, creates a difficult narrative situation. After all, tragedy can only be remedied by redemption, as when Christ, who bore the cross of the human world of sin, comes again. And indeed, the idealization of street queens today has that messianic quality to it. If only we celebrate Saint Sylvia and Saint Marsha properly, the second coming of the trans women of color of Stonewall will redeem us all. Our politics will be saved by invoking trans women of color and acting in their name. We will rescue them from their betrayal in the 1970s by idealizing them.

Or so it seems.

The Black trans woman—and in diluted form, the generic "trans woman of color" uttered by those unwilling to say "Black" —today carries the political desire of intersectional politics. A tragic figure who endures the worst of multiple oppressions, and yet a revolutionary actor whose every breath signals freedom, she is the one in whose name justice will arrive. As a performative subject, her proximity confirms the righteousness of everyone around her. The trans woman of color's subjection is, on this view, simultaneously a call to action and a road map to a better world. The most egregious example is surely the annual hagiographies of Rivera and Johnson. Everyone from mainstream LGBT organizations like Human Rights Campaign to Silicon Valley corporations like Salesforce offer rosy stories during the month of June, claiming that Rivera and Johnson were the foremothers of archconservative phenomena like same-sex marriage or the gig economy.[47]

Confining the trans woman of color to the function of inspiring martyr means that the real women living under that symbolic pressure encounter harsh judgment whenever they stray from their prescribed role. The academic field of queer theory, in one notorious example, cut its teeth in the early 1990s on determining trans women of color's value to be their possibility of overturning gender norms through the failure to conform. Anything else trans women of color wanted out of womanhood was judged as improperly political. The most dramatic entry in this bibliography is Judith Butler's *Bodies That Matter* (1996), where Butler reads Jennie Livingston's popular 1990 documentary about the Black and Brown ball culture of New York City, *Paris Is Burning*.

At the time, Butler was writing against a rash of shallow readings of their landmark book *Gender Trouble* (1990), which had been boiled down by some readers to the idea that gender is a voluntary performance, essentially no different from doing drag. Frustrated with a perception that was nearly the opposite of *Gender Trouble*'s argument, Butler proposed that *Paris Is Burning* depicts the real-world limitations of subverting gender norms—the places where performativity and performance can rigidify oppressive power structures, rather than soften them. In the role of that failure Butler cast Venus Xtravaganza, a trans Latina and one of the subjects of Livingston's documentary.

Xtravaganza was, devastatingly, murdered before the film's release, and Butler utilized her death as evidence for their argument that "sometimes a fatally subversive appropriation takes place" instead of a politically queer one.[48]

In so many words, Butler blamed Xtravaganza for her own death.[49] Xtravaganza's murder at the hands of a male client became *her* "tragic" miscalculation: the cost of wanting to be a real woman, an unqueer desire for something normal. "If Venus wants to become a woman," wrote Butler, "and cannot overcome being a Latina, then Venus is treated by the symbolic precisely the ways in which women of color are treated. Her death thus testifies to a tragic misreading of the social map of power."[50]

Wanting to be with a man, wanting wealth and security—the good life by 1980s American standards—those were desires that Xtravaganza was supposed to refuse because she had been excluded from them, because it was her job to be a model of queer radicalism as a trans woman of color and a sex worker. In refusing to give up the desire to be real, she had to die for it. To be a poor Latina with a penis meant that her desire was too unrealistic, too much the stuff of fantasy, to ever work out in America. Unlike the queer drag queen that so many readers plucked out of *Gender Trouble* (a successor to the drag queens of *Mother Camp*, no doubt), the one who had no wish to be made real, Xtravaganza was supposed to reveal the wishful thinking of a naive politics of performativity.

Butler was roundly critiqued for dismissing the actual circumstances of Xtravaganza's death in favor of a philosophical version of the problem.[51] But the vicious dismissal of Xtravaganza's desire for realness still stings all these decades later, even as Butler is a staunch defender of trans women and an important critic of global anti-trans movements.[52] "Now Venus, Venus Xtravaganza," wrote Butler, "she seeks a certain transubstantiation of gender in order to find an imaginary man who will designate a class and race privilege that promises a permanent shelter from racism, homophobia, and poverty."[53] Why did Butler repeat her name, Venus, twice? It's not just Butler who wrote this way. bell hooks's 1992 essay "Is Paris Burning?" made the same move. hooks called Xtravaganza "Venus" throughout, reserving the honorific of a last name for the film's director, "Livingston."[54] By reading her murder as a theoretical allegory, Butler and hooks wanted Venus Xtravaganza to become one of a million wayward souls caught up in the vast ocean of racial and gendered violence in the Americas. Deprived of her surname, the name of her ballroom house, Xtravaganza became just another Venus, an object lesson to the reader.

Butler and hooks wrote as if Xtravaganza naively said nothing, or knew nothing, of her own life and its dangers, being too caught up in fantasies of realness. In truth, though, she says more than enough in *Paris Is Burning* itself to challenge anyone who would dare speak in her name. Xtravaganza introduces herself with a laugh, saying in her unmistakably soft voice, "I would like to be a spoiled, rich white girl" because "they get what they want, whenever they want it. They don't have to really struggle." Lying in her bed, she looks directly at the camera as she explains, "I don't feel that there's anything mannish about me except maybe what I might have between me down there." "I guess that's why I want a sex change," she explains, "to make me complete." She tells a story of moving to New York as a young teenager, meeting the House of Xtravaganza, and being offered a home without even having to walk in a ball. Venus also pays tribute to her house father, Hector Xtravaganza. On her fifteenth birthday, Hector took Venus to the West Village and threw her a party where she met "a lot of drag queens, transvestites that I didn't believe [were trans] because they were so beautiful, and that kind of sunk into my head." Far from a tragedy foretold by unrealistic fantasy, Xtravaganza came out as a trans teenager in the original sense of the phrase: coming into a preexisting community that cared for her and welcome her into a shared way of life.

There is nothing wishful about Xtravaganza's reflection on sex work, either. She shares a story on screen about a violent client who touched her body and "totally flipped out," screaming: "You fucking faggot! You're a freak! You're a victim of AIDS and you're trying to give me AIDS, what are you crazy? You're a homo, I should kill you." Terrified for her life, Xtravaganza grabbed her bag and jumped out the window. Ever since, she tells Livingston, she prefers to go out on more traditional dates. In fact, she had one the night she was being interviewed. She predicted that after cocktails he would buy her a dress, or maybe some jewelry, "so that the next time he sees me, he'll see me looking more and more beautiful, the way he wants to see me. But I don't have to go to bed with them or anything like that."

Butler faulted Xtravaganza for wanting above all a conventional version of the good life, but in *Paris Is Burning* that desire is spoken explicitly in defiance of a double standard applied to poor trans women. Xtravaganza flipped the terms of the desire, suggesting that wealthy, white, non-trans women were hardly so different from trans sex workers. "If you're married [to] a woman in the suburbs ... and she wants him to buy her a washer and dryer set," she says, "I'm sure she'd have to go to bed with him anyway to give him what he wants for her to get what she wants. So, in the long run, it all ends up the same way." Venus Xtravaganza doesn't apologize for her desire, because she refuses to be demonized for wanting what non-trans women are told is their birthright. "I want this," she says. "This is what I want. And I'm gonna go for it." The camera lingers on her at sunset on the West Side Piers, smoking a cigarette and relaxing, effortlessly beautiful and radiant, as a member of the house of Xtravaganza explains the circumstances of her death. Only those who see no future for women like Venus Xtravaganza, those whose theories of challenging norms rely on the martyrdom of trans women of color, would overlook her sophisticated explanation of the conditions of her life, work, and womanhood to conclude that she died for a naive fantasy.

Nearly thirty years later, the pendulum has swung hard in the opposite direction. Today trans women of color like Xtravaganza are presented not as tragic failures but as near goddesses. In the era of trans hypervisibility, the mere presence of a Black or Brown trans woman is supposed to leap into good politics. The trans woman of color appears as a symbol, invoked as the figure in whose name activism, or intersectional consciousness, is conducted. But the trans woman of color is still just that: a figure for other people. In that sense, surprisingly little has changed since *Paris Is Burning*.

Centering the trans woman of color has not resulted in sustained engagement with her everyday life, expertise, and activism. Had liberal trans-inclusive political movements, or academia, done so, their primary concerns would be prison abolition, police violence, and sex work—not a politics of overcoming the gender binary; and not, at its narrowest, the highly conservative claim that the trans woman of color deserves to be rescued from death.

As trans studies scholars C. Riley Snorton and Jin Haritaworn have argued, this "necropolitical" logic conditioning the circulation of the Black trans woman and the trans woman of color literally needs the material violence it invokes and records.[55] In this economy, the trans woman of color is always a preface to someone else's work, used up in memoriam. She appears this way in one of the foundational texts of queer of color studies, Roderick Ferguson's *Aberrations in Black* (2003), a book that opens with a "black drag-queen prostitute," a passing figure from a scene in Marlon Rigg's 1989 art film *Tongues Untied*. Why, in a film that is a deeply important statement about Black gay men, does Ferguson turn to the one brief appearance of a trans femme? This queen appears midway through *Tongues Untied* with no speaking role. As she wanders a public space and smokes a cigarette, an Essex Hemphill poem is read as the voiceover. The film says nothing direct about who she is, or what her relationship to the Black men in the film might be. Ferguson values her appearance for what it figures, asking, "what mode of analysis would be appropriate for interpreting the drag-queen prostitute as an image that allegorizes and symbolizes that social heterogeneity" of Black life.[56] The words *allegorize* and *symbolize* are key: *Aberrations in Black* does not learn from what this Black trans femme knows or does with the situation of her life, but rather employs her as the precondition for critiquing racial capitalism and establishing intersectional queer studies.[57] Once she has served her figurative purpose in the first few pages of the book, she disappears altogether, much like we are led to believe happens in the film.

Yet to mystify a Black trans femme like this is to refuse to look more closely at *Tongues Untied*. In a 1991 interview in *Afterimage* magazine, Riggs spoke at length about why he cast this queen, a lifelong drag performer from San Francisco who went by many names. Riggs understood her function to be iconic. "I think he represents an icon that we as black gay men—we as gay men, we as people in general tend to dissociate ourselves from," he explains. "As gay men we're othered by the dominant straight society, as black men by white society. And yet, as if to establish our own dominance, our status, we have to other someone else. Drag queens become the baseline beyond which we can't go, because that's really abject."[58] By pairing the Black queen's appearance with the Hemphill poem "Homocide," dedicated to a murdered femme friend, Riggs explained that he meant to "invest the drag queen with a very dignified humanity."[59] When the interviewer asked if "the transvestism in the piece actually speaks about the possible sexual vulnerability of all black gay men," Riggs agreed she responds to "a very visceral need to be loved, as well as a sense of abject loneliness of life where nobody loves you." He felt that the queen's "is not a tragic story but a noble story, a heroic story."

Riggs even agreed with the interviewer's suggestion that the femme might be his alter ego on screen.[60]

The Black queen's appearance in *Tongues United* is hardly as opaque or fleeting as Ferguson implies, but once again she is primarily meaningful for everyone who is not her. Her Black trans femininity and life on the streets make meaning for Riggs as an artist, for Black gay men, for gay men writ large, and for the audience, rather than drawing any of them closer to her. But, by the same token, Riggs embraces the fact that the gay male imaginary has been one of the principal sites for imagining her. Indeed, gay men have depended on street queens like the one featured in *Tongues Untied*, making her presence in the film pivotal, not ornamental.

In honor of the real queens whose lives are so often scrubbed from the images through which they circulate in gay culture, this Black femme queen graces the cover of this book.

Betting on martyrdom and redemption does a disservice to trans women, distancing us from their material struggle. Saint Sylvia and Saint Marsha have become whoever anyone wants them to be, instead of who or what they asked others to think of them. The hagiography, or deification, of the trans women of Stonewall has ironically created more distance from the role they played as queens of the gay world. Their unfinished business has been discarded rather than preserved, no doubt because it contests the privatized, gender-normative mainstreaming of LGBT people that has transpired since the midcentury.

At its root, the redemption of tragedy requires waiting for the creation of a new world, a heaven on earth. The Second Coming requires waiting for utopia in the next life. But the street queen's most urgent cry was not to wait. When she rose in defiance at Cooper's Donuts, Compton's Cafeteria, or Stonewall, she urged everyone to fight now, here on this earth. Her aim was to transform what is already here, instead of hoping that one day the world will be redeemed.

Wisely, then, John Rechy chose not to finish Miss Destiny's story, leaving the ending open in *City of Night*. Destiny doesn't accept the verdict of the evil angel who brings about Judgment Day from a gay bar in downtown Los Angeles. Her speech ends with a far more dramatic upheaval: she indicts God for his inadequacy in the face of her majesty. "There *is* a God," she tells the youngmen and queens in her apartment, "and He is one hell of a joker." Instead of accepting his judgment that she isn't real, or that she should live out the rest of her life in Pershing Square, she announces the ultimate riot. "Im going to storm heaven and protest! *Here I am!!!!!*" Unafraid, she is ready to scream in God's face, who could be no worse than any cop or john who had threatened her a million times. "And god will cringe!"[61]

Rechy's chapter is not titled "The Tragedy of Queen Destiny," after all, but rather "Miss Destiny's Fabulous Wedding." And it ends not with Judgment Day but a sort of anti-ending. The narrator leaves LA for a while. When he returns to Pershing Square, he finds that Destiny has disappeared. No one knows where she went, or what happened to her. He asks around, and the consensus seems to be that she had her dream wedding and then vanished without a trace. But no one knows what happened, because no one showed up to her wedding. The queen's subjects abandoned her in her moment of glory.

Everyone tells the narrator a story that is as true as it is surely false.

Chuck claims first that Destiny had the wedding she had always dreamed of, although he wasn't there to see it. "She had it out in Hollywood, man, in this real fine pad, an I heard she ackshooly dressed like a bride, man."

Pauline tells it differently. "Well, she had her wedding all right, she didn't *invite* me, but I heard, and it was *Hor-ri-bile*." Apparently, Destiny tripped and fell down the winding staircase of the Hollywood mansion in her wedding dress. "Then the place was *raided*" by the vice squad. "And *that's* where Miss Destiny the college co-ed is now, *busted!*—in the *joint—again!*—for *masquerading.*" Pauline asks the youngman to imagine the awful juxtaposition: "Miss Destiny in bridal drag sitting crying in the paddywagon on her *wedding day*."

But Trudi disagrees with both Chuck and Pauline, claiming that Destiny disappeared because she's living happily "in Beverly Hills with the man who sponsored the wedding." Except, Trudi didn't attend the wedding either, afraid of a police raid, so she couldn't be sure.

Chuck supplies a final possibility: that the wedding was entirely the opposite of gay. He says he heard that Destiny's court-ordered psychiatrist from her last arrest had finally succeeded in turning her back into a man, who then married "*a real woman!*" The narrator watches as "Chuck pushed his widehat over his eyes as if to block the sudden vision of a world in which such crazy things can happen."

The narrator doesn't believe any version of the story of Miss Destiny's wedding. And that is precisely why Rechy's account of the queen's reign and fall is not a tragedy. It's more like an instruction: keep the faith, but don't give up the political struggle on which it depends. Perhaps he was reminding the gay world that if no one showed up for their queen, they would ultimately be deprived of her power, though that power could never be extinguished. Perhaps Rechy knew that the queen was the one who held political and spiritual force in trust. In her transubstantiation, the queen held the metaphysical key to the alchemy it would take to lead a movement out of the policing, poverty, and immiseration of their gay lives at the hands of a cruel American society. In being the only one willing to storm heaven and spit in God's face, Miss Destiny wielded a militant, unapologetic power that was abandoned in the aftermath of Stonewall. But it wasn't destined to fail as it would in a Shakespearean tragedy. Things could always have worked out differently. And they still could, in the future.

The street queen's lesson concerns not how to suffer with grace, but what it takes to build a genuinely trans-feminist movement—one that doesn't rely on the fantasy of redemption, letting everyone off the hook for the problems of this world by waiting for the Second Coming of queer utopia. The queen knows best the immense risk and the transformative reward of standing for femininity in this world. The queen is the one ready to take on whoever is holding her back from her divine birthright, whether it be a police officer, middle-class gay activists, or God himself. Perhaps Rechy foresaw that despite Destiny's disappearance, the street queen's crown would be held in trust. Perhaps he knew that her divine body, her political body, would be passed on to successive generations of queens. As the conclusion to this book explores, perhaps the work of queens is inherited today by those fighting in the global South for the political and spiritual value of their unique beauty and power.

Conclusion

Mujerísima and Scarcity Feminism

Two centuries after Mary Jones strolled the streets of New York, trans womanhood remains strangely unthinkable. The girls know *trans* is a word that can be turned against us. We know that trans cultural visibility and its liberal politics thrive on the disavowal, theft, and destruction of our ways of life, and of our dreams. We know this happens especially when we are most visible, at the center of other people's thinking and activism, or even their central concern. When movements claim to act in our name, or use our image as their rallying cry, it is often to imagine a world where trans womanhood is implicitly obsolete, no longer needed in gender's abolition or an infinite taxonomy of individual identities beyond the binary. The use and abuse of trans womanhood secures otherwise-contrary versions of gender-based politics, from intersectional and queer feminism to white women's fascism and Christian fundamentalism. The cavalry in the global gender wars line up on their opposing sides, cannons ablaze, but each agrees not to admit the premise they share: trans femininity is not integral to the future they are fighting for.

Of course, the trans-exclusionary radical feminist (TERF), who lately prefers to go by "gender critical," is most obvious (and obsessive) in this hatred. Like many bad-faith artists, being gender critical means savoring the grift, manufacturing pretenses to prosecute the case against "gender ideology" and rescue its supposed victims. The Bible in this genre, Janice Raymond's *The Transsexual Empire* (1979), detonated a vicious rape metaphor whose impact continues to be felt. The image is of men forcing women, even lesbians, into submission through a technological subterfuge then called transsexuality.[1] Forty years later, not much has changed. The British philosopher Kathleen Stock warns of a "new paradigm, in vogue in many millennial communities," of "what we would ordinarily call heterosexual, or straight" men in lesbian relationships after transitioning. "The rest of us are now urged to accept the phenomenon of a 'lesbian with a penis,'" she cries, "or even a 'girldick.'" Like Raymond, Stock's position is arrogant enough to decide by fiat that there are no trans women; there are only newly fashioned trickster "males" "badgering females for sex," "a familiar phenomenon since time immemorial." Shockingly, it is feminists who are to blame, and they must expel trans women to regain their honor. Stock thinks feminists have been so nice in their embrace of platitudes of inclusion that they have let men engineer the trans conceit. As a result, she claims, "the case for rape by deception is much harder to make."[2] Even consensual lesbian relationships are apparently lies. The trans woman is Stock's predator, but the feminist is also a victim to be blamed.

Gender-critical journalists like Abigail Shrier have contributed to powerful moral panics over trans masculinity. Yet, Shrier condescendingly fantasizes trans boys as savable in adolescence, as pitiable victims of a trend in which "many of the adolescent girls suddenly identifying as transgender seemed to be caught in a 'craze'—a cultural enthusiasm that spreads like a virus."[3] The fantasy of a "craze" implies a new and reversible phenomenon, whereas Stock, like Raymond forty years prior, charges trans women with the original sin of maleness. The strongest vitriol of gender-critical partisans is thus reserved for trans women, remediating Raymond's explosive rhetoric.

Trans misogyny magically converts trans women from the empirically disproportionate recipients of sexual violence into its all-powerful, ontological perpetrators. While trans women are in truth perhaps more than four times as likely to experience intimate violence than non-trans people of all genders, the trans misogynist instead fantasizes that trans women are responsible for that violence simply by existing.[4] This is the logic of trans panic, a legal defense still admissible in most US states through which a defendant can be acquitted for murder, or have their sentence reduced, if they claim to have lost their sanity in a consensual sexual experience with a trans woman.[5]

Trans panic remains a potent idea outside the law because it is circular. On the one hand, it charges that trans women are not women, because their "gender" is really a dangerous sexuality, reducible to an inherently violent penis (though actual men with penises, who outnumber trans women in the world by massive numbers, are conspicuously not the central targets of such TERF campaigns). On the other hand, it claims that non-trans "sexuality" is truthfully a matter of gender (or sex, used synonymously). Women are biologically endangered by penises, and men are driven to legitimate homicidal rage at their sight. When it is convenient, the TERF will ontologize gender as sexuality, turning trans womanhood into a sexual perversion. But, just as soon as it suits her, she will turn around and ontologize sexuality as gender, making non-trans sexuality derivative of immutable manhood or womanhood—of fossilized biological sex. It is, ironically, one of the most ideologically structured accounts of gender to be found anywhere in the world. This closed circuit forms the resilience of trans misogyny, where to be a woman is to be in constant danger and to be a man is to be inherently violent—no exceptions. Such a ghastly definition of feminism is made respectable by blaming trans women for the whole thing.

Once dehumanized, there is no unjust punishment for trans women. Men can avoid prison sentences for killing trans women by invoking the trans panic defense. Gender-critical feminists can calmly call for stripping trans women of their human rights, for mandating state violence against them, or even demand their eradication from the face of the earth—often all in the same breath.[6] The Women's Human Rights Campaign in the UK, for instance, lobbied the government to rescind the Gender Recognition Act, removing civil rights for trans women, and thereby to work toward their elimination from British society. In its submission to the government's inquiry on reforms to the GRA, the WHRC claims that "transgender-ism" "will increase or decrease as a result of social forces," which it names as queer theory, pornography, "the normaliza-tion of men's cross-dressing by medical professionals," and "legal recognition," making it possible to socially eradicate trans people through planned governmental policy. Although this policy would affect all trans people, the specter of trans women's supposed violent tendencies unleashed in bathrooms and prisons—what J. K. Rowling astoundingly contended, in nearly the language of nineteenth-century race scientists, was trans women's "male pattern of criminality"—that has driven the broader political campaign against the GRA.[7]

The TERFs' revanchist designs figure the trans woman as a sexual aggressor deserving of every violence as revenge, sali-vating to gain access to women's spaces and bodies because bleeding-heart liberals are too kind to say no. Their political allies on the right chime in to add that young trans girls must be bullied into submission, chased out of their hometowns, barred from doctor's offices and sport teams, or even abducted from their homes to be placed in foster care or conversion therapy.[8] Shelley Luther, a Republican candidate for the Texas House of Representatives, complained at a campaign event in 2022 that as a former teacher she was no longer allowed to let the children at her school bully trans kids: "I couldn't have kids laugh at them."[9] This symbolic singling out of trans children, especially girls, has many grisly examples. In 2018, after an organized campaign of harassment and threats sur-rounding her attendance at school, the family of a young trans girl in Oklahoma was forced to flee their small town, worried for their safety.[10] In 2021, Arkansas became the first US state to ban gender-affirming care for children, while Mississippi became the first to ban trans girls form participating in school sports. The number of such bills has continued to skyrocket, including a 2021 Texas bill that would have declared affirming a child's gender legal child abuse and allowed the state to take trans children from their homes to place them in the foster care system, where presumably they would be placed with transphobic guardians who could intentionally mistreat them to suppress their gender.[11]

Perhaps the point is to try to stop girls from growing up to be trans women, or maybe the motive is simply to punish them at every opportunity. While trans-masculine or nonbinary people are occasionally deemed rescuable by people like Shrier if they were to renounce and detransition—a horrifically demeaning and genocidal prospect in itself—anti-trans politics has proven itself strident in its goal of eliminating trans womanhood by any means necessary, to the point that when right-wing media targets trans men or trans-masculine people for harassment or misinformation, they often misgender them in a way that implies they are trans women.[12]

The anti-trans pundit class, with its mix of self-identified cancel-culture victims, freelance journalists, and out-of-work male comedians, launders this political extremism with few consequences. QAnon conspiracy theorists, white supremacist militias, Evangelical Christian fascists, and anti-democracy groups anxiously project onto trans women accusations of pedophilia and grooming, openly employ rape and death threats against them, and warn of the end of Western civiliza-tion and empire in a manic relativism of gender ideology.[13] This motley crew, who mix anti-Semitic theories of global Jewish conspiracy with claims that transition is satanic abuse, are politically the gender-critical feminists' best friends.[14] Extremist groups have engaged an informal alliance with anti-trans feminists and pundits, mostly dramatically evidenced by the prominence of Nazis at an Australian rally held by UK anti-trans campaigner Posie Parker.[15] But anti-trans politics are increasingly the glue of a global who's who of authoritarian and ethnonationalist movements from Mexico to Brazil, Canada to France, Poland to Hungary, the Vatican to Russia, and India to the Philippines.[16] In its gender-critical dress-up, the Anglosphere's TERF has gone global, and she has pledged her allegiance to xenophobic and nationalist strongmen, anti-Semites and fundamentalists, without a lick of irony about their beliefs about women, let alone the rest of their political aims. But surely the strangest new bedfellows to these movements are the trans people dedicating themselves to the cause of trans misogyny.

Porn-star-turned-supplements-salesman Buck Angel signed a bizarre open letter with four other trans men in the summer of 2020 denouncing trans womanhood. Endorsing Ray Blanchard's raucously pseudoscientific theory of "autogynephilia" (AGP), in which trans women are somehow perverted heterosexual men aroused by embracing femininity, Angel and his cosignatories claimed that "most of the people at the forefront of trans activism are those heterosexual males with AGP."[17] If trans women weren't really trans, the letter claimed they must instead promote "a sexual orientation." The signatories went on to endorse several gender-critical conspiracy theories, mostly sexual panics. Angel and company conjured fears of sexual predation and claimed that trans women are "behind the transhumanist agenda" that will inevitably destroy the human species. This apocalypse, they claimed, is something for which only trans women are responsible. Announcing themselves by contrast as the true "transgender people with homosexual Gender Dysphoria," Angel and his cowriters explained that they were bravely "taking a stand" and "want our voices heard," although they didn't enumerate any demands.[18] Perhaps attacking trans women was a satisfying end in itself. The only example of political self-harm through trans misogyny more bizarre than Angel's might be Caitlyn Jenner's desire to bar trans girls from playing in organized sports, an irony surely deliverable only in light of her immense wealth and contempt for any politics of material redistribution.[19]

The constellation of anti-trans actors aggressively pursuing political power, within and outside the boundaries of the law, direct their strongest vitriol toward a common target: trans women and trans femininity. This begs a decisive question: How can trans feminism value the very things libeled as sexual pathology, or masculine criminality, and break loose from the logic of eradication? The stakes in answering these questions have never been higher.

Trans women *are* extra. Trans femininity *is* too much. The first mistake of any trans-inclusive feminism is to confine itself by flattening what makes trans femininity and womanhood different from the generic standard. Championing the inclusion of trans women by saying they are indistinguishable from non-trans women is the product of a scarcity mindset. So, too, is claiming that trans femininity has a stable definition or that trans femininity fits neatly into the trans umbrella, or even the LGBT umbrella. Their assimilation into a whole is always a concession to the fear there isn't enough to go around, whether it be money, power, language, or even gender. To make trans-feminist demands smaller in unifying through sameness with non-trans women, or with all trans or LGBT people, is a mistake. In the face of misogyny and the long history of trans-feminization this book has investigated, trans-femininity's positive value calls for a different accounting.

Straight men, gay men, nonbinary people, and non-trans women not only share the world with trans women; they rely on trans femininity to distinguish their genders and sexualities, including through overlap. Gay men's sexual cultures were forged out of the same historical dynamics and urban spaces as trans womanhood. Non-trans women have long shared experiences of downward mobility under marriage and capitalism with trans women, especially in sex work. Many non-trans women have been disqualified from womanhood on anti-Black or racist grounds in ways that make passing for "cisgender" as laughably irrelevant for them as it is for trans women. Straight men, too, depend on the validation of their desire for trans women's femininity to consolidate their manhood. Getting too close to trans femininity, despite its obvious allure, reminds people of their fundamental social interdependence with trans women and trans-feminized people, who have been consigned near to the bottom of most social hierarchies. To hate or dislike trans women, to exclude them, or to attack and scorn trans femininity are all anxious attempts to establish a boundary that violence itself admits never existed in the first place. The trans misogynist constantly confesses her, his, or their inability to escape being in the world with trans women and trans femininity by wishing they could enforce segregation. That's why trans-misogynist violence is so often cruel or subservient to despotic authority. Trans misogyny must hide its fraudulence through overwhelming force. In truth, trans women are not a discrete, separate group of people. Trans femininity is produced out of the collective social body, and like all manifestations of gender, it cannot be isolated and removed from the whole. For those attempting to avoid that inconvenient truth, not much is left other than to accuse trans women of being exceptions: too feminine, too sexual, and too dangerous to live with everyone else.

Trans misogyny often demands the suppression of exceptional femininity, whether to protect someone who is imagined to be in danger or simply to put trans women in their place. That's why trans misogyny fits well into the larger concept of misogyny. Feminist thinkers stress that misogyny often manifests as the policing and isolation of women deemed exceptional or improper in their womanhood. Accordingly, women who are cast as too sexual and too feminine are diminished and imputed by right-wing authoritarians and feminists alike. They are blamed for almost anything, from economic crises to climate change. And often they are found responsible for the very violence they disproportionately experience, whether police brutality, incarceration, poverty, or sexual assault and rape. Trans misogyny shares this key quality of exceptionalizing and blaming sexuality and femininity. Misogyny is a problem that non-trans and trans women share, although it manifests differently. Trans misogyny, for one, is deeply entwined with homophobia, as the intimacy between trans panic and gay panic reminds. What's common across homophobia, trans misogyny, and misogyny directed at non-trans women is the targeting and suppression of femininity as excessive. Feminizing people, regardless of how they see themselves, is the pretext for dehumanizing them.

Misogyny's hatred of femininity means that trans feminism is an urgent project, as trans-feminized people know the promise and fallout of femininity as well as anyone. To that end, this book concludes by uplifting the excess attributed to trans women and trans femininity. What if feminists didn't reply to the charge that trans women are too sexual, or too feminine, by shrinking trans femininity to prove the accuser's bad faith wrong? What if trans feminism meant saying yes to being too much, not because everyone should become more feminine, or more sexual, but because a safer world is one in which there is nothing wrong with being extra? Abundance might be a powerful concept in a world organized by a false sense of scarcity. What if trans feminism dedramatized and celebrated trans femininity as the most feminine, or trans women as the most women? How might trans women lead a coalition in the name of femininity, not to replace or even define other kinds of women, but to show what the world might look like for everyone if it were hospitable to being extra and having more than enough?

Many of the key achievements of liberal feminism, particularly in the West, have relied on minimizing, if not rejecting or trying to transcend, femininity. To achieve equality with men, liberal feminism has often claimed that women are the same as men, downplaying their femininity to adapt to the default masculine model of authority and respect. (This is also why feminists are often charged by misogynists with being too masculine or becoming manly.) Having been typecast as irrational, ornamental, and unserious, femininity is treated as an obstacle to women's equality. Think of how often women politicians are encouraged to project cold, stern public personae, acting like the men in their midst, which in turn becomes proof that they are untrustworthy or inauthentic. And think of how often people associated with the stigma of femininity, like gay men, are encouraged to minimize their femininity to assume public roles or be taken seriously—or even to be granted human rights. The respectability strategy sacrifices femininity to curry favor with dominant, misogynist ideas of power. Whether or not it succeeds in any of its goals, it always extends the devaluation and hatred of femininity. In that way, it always loses.

Who will be bold enough to reclaim femininity in its most excessive, extra forms? Who will proclaim a post-scarcity feminism that isn't afraid of being too much and wanting too much? That possibility is already here in burgeoning trans-feminist movements in Latin America, where one word announces a different path: *mujerísima*.

Mujerísima is a Spanish neologism formed of *mujer* (woman) and the superlative -*ísima*, which denotes the highest degree of something. (In Portuguese, the word is *mulheríssima*.) More elegant when untranslated, it might be rendered in English as "extremely woman" or "the most woman." In Latin America, a *mujerista* is a follower of a liberationist theology that prioritizes women's experiences and power, drawing on a wide array of belief systems from the Caribbean to the Southern Cone.[20] As a *travesti* word, *mujerísima* has a different emphasis. Luciana, a travesti from northeastern Brazil, shared in an interview in the late 1990s that her high femininity made her feel *mulheríssima* with the men in her life. The ethnographer listening translated the word as "like a total woman" but stressed that Luciana's sense of womanhood was not based on assimilation into the generic norm.[21] Leaning into its suffix, *mujerísima* underlines a fierce commitment to being unabashedly the most feminine, or the womanliest of all, in a loudly travesti way, manifestly different from the normative ideal of womanhood. *Mujerísima* is part of a travesti rejection of assimilation, including into transgender womanhood. In Latin America, home to trans-feminist traditions stretching back decades, *mujerísima* can be spoken with a trans-feminist inflection.[22]

Travestis deserve comprehensive, transnational histories of their own that have yet to be written. Travesti is a vast category of identity, culture, class, and politics that differs throughout Latin America. Notably, travesti is *not* a Spanish or Portuguese translation of transgender. Not only does travesti precede transgender by decades; it often challenges, competes with, or outright opposes transgender (*transgénero* in Spanish and *transgênero* in Portuguese) and transsexual (*transexual* in both languages). The term *travesti* was important in Spain under the fascist dictatorship that lasted until the 1970s, and it had resonance in France among radical gay liberation activists.[23] It was also used by twentieth-century anthropologists, often interchangeably with the English words *transvestite* and *transvestism*, flattening cultural differences.[24] But in a Latin American context, travesti has its own meanings. It's strongly racialized, especially in Brazil, where travesti bears a rich Black heritage. There are also a multitude of Indigenous inflections to *travestismo* that texture how people live in the category from region to region. It also correlates strongly to class, emanating from the poorest and most disenfranchised.[25]

Travesti is a vernacular category of trans femininity, meaning it isn't subservient to medical textbooks or other self-appointed experts. It coexists alongside imported concepts like transgender and transsexual, as well as other vernaculars like *transformista*.[26] Perhaps the most significant travesti challenge to the global hegemony of transgender is a refusal to drive a wedge between gender and sexuality. As this book has shown, that division has long been irrelevant in the working classes and outside the metropoles of the global North. Separating gay men from trans femininity is the mission of an intrusive, NGO-driven gentrification of identity politics beginning in the 1990s. Travestis frequently conceive of themselves through sexuality and often prioritize their overlap with gay cultures. Their historical confinement to the service economy, especially sex work, joins them to other trans-feminized people this book has considered. The experience of criminalization and poverty has also structured travesti aesthetics and embodiment. *Mujerísima* is in part a recognition of the high femininity many travestis seek without reference to the Western transgender model. Silicone injections are as quintessentially travesti as hormones, though the point is that there is no single model for travesti femininity and sexuality. Taking real pleasure in a trans-feminine body—affirming the desire to be feminine, to be desired by men, or to enjoy having sex—is quite different from the sober diagnosis of gender dysphoria.

"Travesti is not woman and is not trans," writes Peruvian scholar Malú Machuca Rose.

> Travesti is classed and raced: it means you do not present femininely all of the time because you cannot afford to. It means the use of body technologies to transform one's body does not come from a doctor's office but from resourcefulness in the face of *precarización* … It means you get creative, you use pens for eyeliner, get your hormones and silicones from your friends underground, or use *tinta* instead of *testosterona* to transform

your body. It also means you're only safe at night, when the children are sleeping and the darkness allows a certain freedom and permissiveness to roam more freely.

As Rose sees it, "Travesti is the refusal to be trans, the refusal to be woman, the refusal to be intelligible."[27]

This defiant ethos comes from a history of being targets of state violence, especially in countries that have experienced long periods of dictatorship. Police raids, forced disappearance, and death squads mark the historical memory of many travesti communities, particularly in Brazil, Chile, and Argentina. And when new democratic states have established truth and reconciliation processes, travestis have often been excluded from recognition. In fact, democracy has been continuous in many practical ways with dictatorship. In Chile, as scholars Hilary Hiner and Juan Carlos Garrido explain, Article 373—which authorized extreme police abuse—was not repealed at the end of dictatorship. As a result, "the democratic transitions of the 1990s did not significantly change the situation of trans and travesti women."[28] This unrelenting state violence has manifested a unique political identification as travesti. Writing about Brazil, Dora Silva Santana explains that "*travesti* is an identification that indexes a political position of resistance by trans femme/feminine/women's bodies of, historically, mostly black and people of color from poor communities."[29] The travesti political movement in Brazil has been driven by resistance to police violence, especially in its effects on sex workers.

Travesti political organizing has also challenged the global export of the American model of state recognition and gender-based human rights, and its positioning as if it were a universal good. Far from a neutral extension of the trans umbrella, the internationalization of trans more often serves to steamroll over the lives and concerns of people who don't live up to a middle-class, whitewashed, or Western ideal of gender identity subservient to the state. Writing about Peru, Rose explains that "in contrast to the supposed universality of trans, travesti is provincialized and particular."[30] Perhaps the strongest travesti critiques have been of the human rights framework of gender self-identification or self-determination, most famously articulated in the Yogyakarta Principles.[31] In Argentina, travesti activists were pivotal critics of the country's 2012 Gender Identity Law (LIG), which allowed gender markers on national ID documents to be changed through self-identification, loosening requirements, but only for a binary of M and F. The law also guaranteed access to medical care for transition, a major shift in state policy. The LIG is now joined by countless other laws around the world that prioritize self-ID as the signal measure of trans human rights—although self-ID is in political trouble in the UK and the US.[32]

Travesti activists raised the alarm that the LIG in fact legally erased them. By reinforcing the practice of "man" and "woman" as the only gender markers on documents, travestis had no way to be recognized and continued to face the material fallout of not having workable ID. Given the poverty and criminalization they face in Argentina, the law reinforced travesti immiseration instead of alleviating it, making it even harder to access public benefits, resist police violence, and work in the formal economy. By tying the relaxation of self-ID to the adoption of the Yokyakarta Principles, the Argentinian state also codified a preference for the medical subject of gender dysphoria—a subject who could be reformed into health and compliance. This new transgender citizen exists in contrast with the ongoing moralizing and policing of travestis as public health threats, or sexual threats to the nation itself. But travesti activists did not ask for a reform of the law to include them, say, with an "X" option for IDs; instead, they challenged the very legitimacy of state power to regulate gender and sexuality. They did not want to be coerced into gendered citizenship at all. As the activist Marlene Wayar put it, "We *travestis* are not men or women; we are constructions of personal substance, our own absolutely and highly personal body of laws."[33]

If the democratic state, like the dictatorial state, targets travestis' "personal body of laws," then Wayar imagines a politics that does not seek the state's blessing for legitimacy. The mujerísima targeted by both the dictatorial and democratic state generates a much better travesti concept of freedom from regulation and policing, abandoning the reform of inherently harmful state power. Unlike the international trans politics that homogenize and flatten different ways of life, Wayar doesn't demand perfection or unity in this vision of trans feminism. Her concept of political action isn't predicated on finding the right language, or the right identities, to include everyone in their imagined proper place. Instead of demanding that every individual be obligated to find their true self and present it to the state for evaluation, this version of travesti politics rejects the project of idealism and its impossible search for a home in language or law. Wayar takes the angle of *lo suficientemente bueno*—"the good enough." She borrows the phrase from the psychoanalyst Donald Winnicott, who in the 1960s described "the good-enough mother" as warm and empathetic. Instead of straining to appear without flaws and erasing herself to meet every whim of her child, the good-enough mother provides more than enough by embracing her imperfection, teaching her child an important lesson in ambiguity. In Wayar's hands, the good enough begins as a travesti theory for change and abundance without perfection—a proposition good enough to move people to action, to finding something safer and happier than the subservience demanded by the state.[34]

Strange as it may seem, the maximalism of mujerísima fits into the modest principle of *lo suficientemente bueno*. Wayar frames travesti political organizing as fundamentally materialist. Action emanates from the shared inadequacy and poverty of everyday life, rather than abstract fables of human rights and state recognition based on arbitrary ideas of deserving and undeserving citizens. Instead of medical gender identities or legal recognition of LGBT citizens, Wayar's good-enough questions for organizing are simple: "Why do we have to live everyday with fear? Why do we have to go home afraid?"[35] Answering them would take a coalition, a trans feminism that knits together travestis with everyone else who finds common cause in ensuring that everyone has a good-enough life. In the place of taxonomies that separate travestis from other women, Wayar imagines the work of *convivencia*—living peacefully across difference, where collective flourishing doesn't require the adoption of a singular model and its imposition on everyone. "Unfortunately," she explains of the present world, "we are in coexistence. There is a huge difference between coexistence and convivencia."[36]

Travesti politics, in Wayar's terms, are about what's good enough for everyone, not perfection for some and suffering for others. She advises queer, trans, and feminist movements to give up the quest for the perfect language, or law, to govern identity. The good enough keeps us present, attuned to what is here in the world, instead of asking to wait for our reward until we find perfection or utopia. And what is already here is the grace, divinity, and power of our queens.

In the music video for "Mulher" (2017), the Brazilian artist Linn da Quebrada glimpses a travesti politics of the most *mulher* (woman). The song follows Quebrada narrating the night as a *trava feminina* working the street. Sparkling under streetlights in heels and a silver-sequined bikini top, jacket, and shorts, Quebrada gets into the car of a client while the lyrics proclaim her sovereignty as diva of the gutter. By marketing her body to men of every class, from poor to rich, they become indebted to her, even if she, in turn, needs their money to purchase her body back on her own terms. The camera begins to wander in the night, spreading out from Quebrada to other travestis leaving jobs to find one another. Relaxing together, smoking a cigarette, or having a drink, the sisterhood they knit on the street is given lilting form in the chorus, as Quebrada draws out the word *mulher* over and over.[37]

The song takes on a drumbeat at this point to signal a militant shift. The travestis assemble under the call of mulher, but Quebrada reminds that they are not seeking to be erased via inclusion in anything generically woman. They may have an abundance of face, curves, breasts, and ass, but she sings just as proudly of their *pau de mulher* (woman's cock) in the same breath. And that difference, that unashamed excess of sexuality and femininity, challenges their current value on the street. The usual arithmetic of one man with one woman doesn't exist in this economy. It was replaced long ago, sings Quebrada, by ten travestis to a single paying man. The gap between their aesthetic triumph as the pinnacle of femininity and their treatment as dirty secrets by men is what generates their concrete struggle.

In a stunningly choreographed scene, Quebrada arrives at the quiet street where a client has taken her, and, a little forcefully, pulls her from the car. She is pushed up against a brick wall, and the camera fuzzes out slightly as it zooms in, no longer able to capture all of what's happening. Maybe he pushed her, but then again, maybe she thrust herself. Close up shots follow her nails tracing the side of the wall while she moans so ambivalently it's impossible to tell how much of Quebrada's performance signifies pleasure and how much is expressing pain. The way her lacquered nails glide off the wall and under her shorts, digging deep, suggests she's immersed in herself. A second scene is intercut with this one, where two men are physically overwhelming her more obviously, coming close to choking her as they make to fuck her. Flashing back to the previous location, the camera lingers on Quebrada's mouth as she screams out, again confusing whether she is crying in suffering or in ecstasy. The impossibility of detangling the force of travesti sexuality—the pleasure of being too much a woman—from trans-misogynist violence and the conditions of criminalized sex work cancels any wish to moralize what is happening on screen.

As Quebrada sings her love for the way travestis fight, the camera shifts to an empty intersection where three groups of travestis converge and retake the street in the name of their "right to live, shine, and slay" (*direito de viver brilhar e arrasar*). The group marches to find Quebrada being held down by men on the hood of a car, struggling to escape. They rush to her, ripping the men away as she sings that she is running from a certain kind of man, the man who consumes and then disappears, content only to take what he wants—to fuck and then run away. Repeating the word *some* (vanish) so that it changes from a description of that man to an instruction (go away!), even an incantation, the song ends—but the video has an epilogue.

In the light of day, the community of travestis that saved Quebrada now sit tightly knit in white fabric, bathing and conferring affection on one another in an anointed ceremony. As they embrace, hold each other close, and run their hands along each other's bodies and faces with sweetness, the refrain "I'm running from a man" (*Eu tô correndo de homem*) hums first as a chant, or a prayer, before it becomes an expressive, bounding note of joy. Clapping and singing in a chorus, the women's infectious smiles fill the frame. The epilogue expresses what Santana calls *mais viva*! (more alert or alive): "that embodied knowledge developed within that liminal space of not forgetting the imbrications between experiences of violence and the ways we find joy and acknowledgement and support, even if that comes in a micro-intimate level." *Mais viva* "is not just being alive *but more alive*."[38] Telling a story revolving around Afro-Brazilian travestis, Quebrada stresses that they know how to be more alive, to live the most of anyone, but that this is no tragedy. They may live out a heightened exposure to premature death, but it can't be pulled apart from their capacity to reach even higher exaltation and pleasure in superlative living.

Like much of Quebrada's work, "Mulher" has no time for shyness and even less for wishful moralizing. Digging deep into the volatile convergence of pleasure and pain, particularly in its blasphemous resonance, Quebrada does not shrink the travesti demand on the category mulher to gain admission to its charmed circle. She revels in the ecstasy of being too much, or the most woman, because that is what makes her proudest to be travesti. It's what led her to desire a body and social world greater than anything offered. This she shows without splitting that superiority from the working conditions and the men who antagonize sex workers. It's the collective embrace of mulheríssima that grants the power to break Quebrada out of a dangerous situation, but also to assemble for love and healing in the wake of violence. The video witnesses a transfiguration taking place, in all its Afro-diasporic reworking of Catholicism. The heightened danger of being desired and punished for being too much, for being *trava*, is not cast off out of fear. It is made to secure a different order of divinity. Anyone who doubts that power need only listen to the song's epilogue, letting it saturate your flesh and bones—or gaze upon the smiling faces of Quebrada and her sisters, who wear a certainty in their joy earned only in the rarest of circumstances. This is not the stuff of subversion, or utopia, or alternative social structures. It is richly real and beyond domestication into a universal theory of gender.

"Mulher" announces that the kingdom of the queens is not what awaits in heaven after a pious lifetime of suffering and tragedy. Femininity *is* the reward, here and now. Sexuality signals its arrival in the fleshy present. Heaven is already here on earth, growing with each demonstration in the streets and each ceremonial commitment to the sanctity of travesti femininity in shades richly Black and Brown, linking with the struggles of non-travesti women who have been policed by misogyny and racism. Strangely, wondrously, the travesti politics of the good enough, though they set aside the impossible threshold of perfection, are nothing like pragmatism. What's good enough is not predetermined or static, which means it has no limit. What's good enough can grow and change over time, without a prescribed end, meaning it can deliver on the vastness of mujerísima. What proves to be good enough for travestis, for trans-feminized people around the world, and for the divinity of trans femininity itself, is nothing less than the most.

Will you demand it all?

Acknowledgments

This book began a thousand times before I wrote a single word, born of the agony of frustration that trans women know too well: being aggressed at every turn long before we sense our power. But it also had a fateful, concrete beginning when my incomparable editor, Rosie Warren, wrote me for a chat. Her intuition that a book was brewing in my public speaking and writing about trans misogyny was a happy occasion during a difficult period, when I was otherwise moving to a new city, starting a new job, starting over in a world forever restructured by the COVID-19 pandemic, and being thrown into the rising tide of anti-trans fascism to boot. Rosie not only foresaw this book but guided the manuscript into its present form with a singular wisdom about how to realize its many aspirations. All the shortcomings to be found in these pages remain mine.

I have been remarkably lucky to develop the thinking and storytelling that comprises this book in concert with countless generous audiences. The book's eventual critical edge emerged in delivering the 2021 Queer Theory Lecture at Duke University, while the first occasion to speak to its historiography was the University of Calgary's Annual LGBTQS2+ Lecture a year later. Rewarding time spent at the University of Southern California's Consortium for Gender, Sexuality, Race, and Public Culture as a Mellon public scholar in residence, and at the University of California, Irvine, delivering a critical theory lecture series, proved pivotal to the book's development. So, too, was feedback at the University of Washington, Boston University, Columbia University, Brandeis University, Rutgers University, Stanford University, the Leslie Lohman Museum, the University of Utah, the Thinking Trans / Trans Thinking Conference, Exeter University, the University of Virginia, New York University, Princeton University, the University of Mississippi, and the Thinking Gender conference at the University of California, Los Angeles.

I owe much to intrepid and inventive students at Johns Hopkins, especially the PhD students in my seminar "The History of Trans Femininity," where we dared to cocreate an object of study and methodology simultaneously by reading impossibly widely. Students in successive semesters of "The Gender Binary and American Empire" also impressed on me the rewards of thinking much bigger than the *trans* in trans studies ordinarily would.

This is my first book-length attempt to write for more than an academic audience. The opportunity to try reflects transformative bonds I share with so many of you. The *Death Panel* community has invited me to fearlessly use my voice and has reminded me why we stay alive another week, every week: to learn to want more out of the world. The wide web of interlocutors I've met through writing for the internet, podcasts, and film, especially through *Sad Brown Girl*, *Framing Agnes*, *Outward*, and yes, even trans Twitter, have each meant a lot to me.

I find myself enjoying an abundance of love beyond my wildest dreams, without which I simply wouldn't have what it takes to write about trans misogyny. Thank you to my nearest and dearest: Jean-Thomas Tremblay, who also read the entire manuscript; Syd Gill, who makes me the luckiest sister in the world; and Kadji Amin, who has shown me, in its glorious profundity, what it means to love a trans woman without reservation, with the joy of all its divine possibility—*gracias, papi, te adoro.*

Notes

Introduction

1 For an overview of the various ways in which trans has come to circulate in contemporary thought, see Susan Stryker, "Introduction: Trans* Studies Now," *TSQ: Transgender Studies Quarterly* 7, no. 3 (2020): 299–305.

2 Leslie Feinberg, "Transgender Liberation: A Movement Whose Time Has Come" (1992), *Workers World*, November 2, 2017, workers.org.

3 David Valentine, *Imagining Transgender: An Ethnography of a Category* (Durham, NC: Duke University Press, 2007), 4.

4 Ibid., 4.

5 "Easy Come, Easy Go," *Sex and the City*, season 3, episode 9, HBO, aired August 6, 2000.

6 Chris Burns, "5 Episodes of 'Sex and the City' That Are Now Cringeworthy," *Betches*, August 21, 2019, betches.com.

7 See *Disclosure*, directed by Sam Feder (Netflix: 2020).

8 "Violence against Trans and Non-binary People," *VAWnet*, National Resource Center on Domestic Violence, 2021, vawnet.org.

9 Ivan Natividad, "Why Is Anti-trans Violence on the Rise in America?," *Berkeley News*, June 25, 2021, news.berkeley.edu.

10 National Center for Transgender Equality, *Responding to Hate Crimes: A Community Resource Manual*, transequality.org.

11 "Fighting Anti-trans Violence," Lambda Legal, lambdalegal.org.

12 "Fatal Violence against the Transgender and Gender Nonconforming Community in 2022," Human Rights Campaign, 2022, hrc.org; Madeleine Carlisle, "Anti-trans Violence Reached Record Highs across American in 2021," *Time*, December 30, 2021, time.com.

13 "Learn More About Hate Crimes in the United States," Department of Justice, justice.gov.

14 Malaika Fraley, "Gwen Araujo Murder 14 Years Later: Transgender Teen's Killers Face Parole," *Santa Cruz Sentinel*, October 14, 2016, santacruzsentinel.com.

15 Gayle Salamon, *The Life and Death of Latisha King: A Critical Phenomenology of Transphobia* (New York: New York University Press, 2018), 1–4.

16 Ibid., 5.

17 "Brandon McInerney Sentenced to 21 Years, Lawyer Says He's Sorry for Killing Classmate," *KPCC*, December 19, 2011, archive. kpcc.org.

18 Julia Serano, *Whipping Girl: A Transsexual Woman on Sexism and the Scapegoating of Femininity* (Berkeley, CA: Seal Press, 2007), 248.

19 Talia Mae Bettcher, "Evil Deceivers and Make-Believers: On Transphobic Violence and the Politics of Illusion," *Hypatia* 22, no 3 (2007): 54.

20 Kate Manne, *Down Girl: The Logic of Misogyny* (Oxford: Oxford University Press, 2018), 32, 53, 24.

21 Jacqueline Rose, *On Violence and On Violence against Women* (New York: Farrar, Straus & Giroux, 2021), 3, 10.

22 I am adapting the kind of analysis developed for the history of sexuality by Christopher Chitty in *Sexual Hegemony*, ed. Max Fox (Durham, NC: Duke University Press, 2020), 24–32.

23 Jennie June, *The Female-Impersonators: A Sequel to the Autobiography of an Androgyne and an Account of Some of the Author's Experiences during His Six Years' Career as Instinctive Female-Impersonator in New York's Underworld* (New York: Medico-legal Journal, 1922), 130–1.

24 Jamie Wareham, "375 Transgender People Murdered in 2021— 'Deadliest Year' since Records Began," *Forbes*, November 11, 2021, forbes.com.

25 For a good overview of the question of trans existence prior to the modern era, see Great LaFleur, Masha Raskolnikov, and Anna Klosowska, "Introduction: The Benefits of Being Trans Historical," in *Trans Historical: Gender Plurality before the Modern* (Ithaca, NY: Cornell University Press, 2021), 1–26.

26 This has long been a point of contention in the LGBT press. For an early discussion, see Ramón A. Gutiérrez, "Must We Deracinate Indians to Find Gay Roots?," *Out/Look* (Winter 1989): 62–7.

27 On the *'aqi*, see Deborah A. Miranda, "Extermination of the Joyas: Gendercide in Spanish California," *GLQ: A Journal of Lesbian and Gay Studies* 16, no. 1 (2010): 253–84. On *renyao*, see Howard Chiang, "Titrating Transgender: Archiving Taiwan through *Renyao* History," in *Transtopia in the Sinophone Pacific* (New York:

Columbia University Press, 2021), 97–136. On *fa'afafine*, see Dan Taulapapa McMullin, *"Fa'afafine* Notes: On Tagaloa, Jesus, and Nafanua," in *Queer Indigenous Studies: Critical Interventions in Theory, Politics, and Literature*, ed. Qwo-Li Driskill et al. (Tucson: University of Arizona Press, 2011), 81–96.

28 This process has been called, in part, a gendercide. See Miranda, "Extermination of the *Joyas*."

29 Gayatri Reddy, *With Respect to Sex: Negotiating Hijra Identity in South India*, 1st ed. (Chicago: University of Chicago Press, 2005); Vaibhav Saria, *Hijras, Lovers, Brothers: Surviving Sex and Poverty in Rural India* (New York: Fordham University Press, 2021).

30 Quoted in Kyla Schuller, *The Trouble with White Women: A Counterhistory of Feminism* (New York: Bold Type, 2021), 187.

31 Finn Enke, "Collective Memory and the Transfeminist 1970s: Toward a Less Plausible History," *TSQ: Transgender Studies Quarterly* 5, no. 1 (2018): 9–29.

32 Schuller, *White Women*, 197–8.

1. The Global Trans Panic

1 Jessica Hinchy, *Governing Gender and Sexuality in Colonial India: The Hijra, c. 1850–1900* (New York: Cambridge University Press, 2019), 34–5.

2 F. Baltazard Solvyns, *Les Hindous, ou description de leurs moeurs, coûtumes, et cérémonies*, vol. 2 (Paris: Imprimerie de Mame Frères, 1810), 140–1.

3 Hinchy, *Governing Gender*, 140–51.

4 Vaibhav Saria, *Hijras, Lovers, Brothers: Surviving Sex and Poverty in Rural India* (New York: Fordham University Press, 2021).

5 Quoted in Hinchy, *Governing Gender*, 33.

6 Philippa Levine, *Prostitution, Race and Politics: Policing Venereal Disease in the British Empire* (New York: Routledge, 2003).

7 Hinchy, *Governing Gender*, 37.

8 Quoted in ibid., 2.

9 Ibid., 63, 108, 101.

10 Ibid., 69, 112–14.

11 Quoted in ibid., 51.

12 Ibid., 57–60.

13 Ibid., 175, 190, 195, 201.

14 Saria, *Hijras, Lovers, Brothers*, 1–24.

15 Quoted in Walter L. L. Williams, *Spirit and the Flesh: Sexual Diversity in American Indian Culture* (Boston: Beacon Press, 1992), 180.

16 For a long view of the gendercide against Two-Spirit peoples

throughout the Americas, see Deborah A. Miranda, "Extermination of the Joyas: Gendercide in Spanish California," *GLQ: A Journal of Lesbian and Gay Studies* 16, no. 1 (2010): 253–84.

17 Timothy J. Gilfoyle, *City of Eros: New York City, Prostitution, and the Commercialization of Sex, 1790–1920*, rev. ed. (New York: W. W. Norton & Company, 1994), 211.

18 Jennie June, *The Female-Impersonators: A Sequel to the Autobiography of an Androgyne and an Account of Some of the Author's Experiences during His Six Years' Career as Instinctive Female-Impersonator in New York's Underworld* (New York: *Medico-legal Journal*, 1922), 130–1.

19 June, *Female-Impersonators*, 131.

20 See *Disclosure*, directed by Sam Feder (Netflix: 2020).

21 June, *Female-Impersonators*,132. The murders would seem to fall into the pattern of violence of which the historian George Chauncey gives a thorough account in *Gay New York: Gender, Urban Culture, and the Making of the Gay Male World, 1890–1940* (New York: Basic Books, 2019).

22 June, *Female-Impersonators*, 138, 140.

23 Ibid., 141.

24 Ibid.

25 Ibid., 142–3.

26 Chauncey, *Gay New York*.

27 Quoted in Allen Drexel, "Before Paris Burned: Race, Class, and Male Homosexuality on the Chicago South Side, 1935–1960," in *Creating a Place for Ourselves: Lesbian, Gay, and Bisexual Community Histories*, ed. Genny Beeman (New York: Routledge, 1997), 125.

28 For the example of Berlin, see Robert Beachy, *Gay Berlin: Birthplace of a Modern Identity* (New York: Vintage, 2015).

29 On the misattribution of male homosexuality to trans-feminine historical figures, see Jules Gill-Peterson, *Histories of the Transgender Child* (Minneapolis: University of Minnesota Press, 2018), 13–15. The next chapter further explores this problem of historical interpretation in an even earlier period through the story of Mary Jones.

30 For the example of London, see Matt Houlbrook, *Queer London: Perils and Pleasures in the Sexual Metropolis, 1918–1957* (Chicago: University of Chicago Press, 2006), 145–6.

31 Quoted in Chauncey, *Gay New York*, 69.

32 Ibid.

33 Chicago, for instance, had well-known "boy houses" by the 1880s. St. Sukie de la Croix, *Chicago Whispers: A History of LGBT Chicago before Stonewall* (Madison: University of Wisconsin Press, 2012), 21.

NOTES FROM PAGES 44 TO 62

34 Ibid., 44–8.
35 Jim Elledge, *The Boys of Fairy Town: Sodomites, Female Impersonators, Third-Sexers, Pansies, Queers, and Sex Morons in Chicago's First Century* (Chicago: Chicago Review Press, 2018), 17.
36 Drexel, "Before Paris Burned," 124, 129.
37 Ibid., 129.
38 Ibid., 130.
39 Ibid.
40 Meredith Talusan, "How the Killing of a Trans Filipina Woman Ignited an International Incident," *Vice*, February 23, 2015, vice.com.
41 Ibid.
42 Mark Joseph Stern, "Marine Who Allegedly Killed Trans Woman Claims He Was Defending His Honor," *Slate*, August 25, 2015, slate.com.
43 *Call Her Ganda*, directed by PJ Raval (2018).
44 Sabrina Rubin Erdely, "The Transgender Crucible," *Rolling Stone*, July 30, 2014, rollingstone.com.
45 CeCe McDonald, "Go Beyond Our Natural Selves: The Prison Letters of CeCe McDonald," ed. Omise'eke Natasha Tinsley, *TSQ: Transgender Studies Quarterly* 4, no. 2 (2017): 258.
46 Erdely, "Transgender Crucible."
47 McDonald, "Go Beyond," 258.
48 Ibid., 260.
49 Ibid., 259.
50 Jason Gutierrez, "Duterte Pardons U.S. Marine Who Killed Transgender Woman, *New York Times*, September 7, 2020, nytimes.com.
51 For an overview of anti-sex-work feminism, and pro-trans critiques of the same, see Juno Mac and Molly Smith, *Revolting Prostitutes: The Fight for Sex Workers' Rights* (New York: Verso, 2018).
52 Julian Kevon Glover, "Customer Service Representatives: Sex Work among Black Transgender Women in Chicago's Ballroom Scene," *South Atlantic Quarterly* 120, no. 3 (2021): 554–5.
53 Quoted in ibid., 563.

2. Sex and the Antebellum City

1 Stephen Mihm, *A Nation of Counterfeiters: Capitalists, Con Men, and the Making of the United States* (Cambridge, MA: Harvard University Press, 2007), 9–11.
2 Timothy J. Gilfoyle, *City of Eros: New York City, Prostitution, and the Commercialization of Sex, 1790–1920*, rev. ed. (New York: W. W. Norton & Company, 1994), 82–3.

3 This rendering of the story is deliberately based on coverage in the *New York Herald* and the *New York Sun*, whose differing details—and penchant for invention—are examined in Jonathan Ned Katz, *Love Stories: Sex between Men before Homosexuality* (Chicago: University of Chicago Press, 2001), 80–2. In this chapter, however, I strongly contest Katz's odd characterization of Jones as a man who dressed as a woman merely for sexual gratification—a claim for which there is absolutely no evidence. Katz's recruitment of Jones for a history of male homosexuality seems rather wishful and loose as historical interpretation. It reflects a generation of gay historians who projected their own sexual categories backward onto people in the past, rather than genuinely historicizing sexuality and gender.

4 However, exhaustive and enterprising research by Riah Lee Kinsey has helped to corroborate, with police and court records, some of the details reported in the penny press, such as the entrapment scheme and the ensuing arrest by Bowyer. Riah Lee Kinsey, "The People vs Mary Jones: Rethinking Race, Sex, and Gender through 19th-Century Court Records," NYC Department of Records and Information Services, August 5, 2022, archives.nyc.

5 *People v. Sewally*, June 16, 1836, Court of General Sessions, New York, County DA Indictment Records, MN#5166, Roll #166, New York City Municipal Archives.

6 Discussing the trial records of the Court of General Sessions, historian Shane White explains that free Black voices "come to us in the form of paraphrases and summaries, larded with the occasional direct quotes, underscore[ing] the extent to which blacks were second-class citizens, compelled to speak but having no control over what was done to their words. The clearest example of this heavy editing is contained in the most plentiful source of material on the lives of African New Yorkers in the early decades of the nineteenth century—the thousands of depositions from blacks taken by the district attorney, depositions that are housed today in the city's Municipal Archives." Shane White, *Stories of Freedom in Black New York* (Cambridge, MA: Harvard University Press, 2002), 10.

7 Quoted in Katz, *Love Stories*, 82.

8 Quoted in ibid., 83.

9 See Gilfoyle, *City of Eros*, 92–9; and Marilynn Wood Hill, *Their Sisters' Keepers: Prostitution in New York City, 1830–1870* (Berkeley, CA: University of California Press, 1993), 10.

10 Henry R. Robinson, "The Man-Monster," lithograph, 1836, Smithsonian National Museum of American History, DL.60.2363.

11 See, for example, John McGinn, *Ten Days in the Tombs; or, A Key to the Modern Bastille* (New York: P. F. Harris, 1855), 56–7.

12 See for example, "Beefsteak Pete Arrested," *National Police Gazette*, March 4, 1858; and an untitled item beginning, "Peter Sewally, alias Ann Eliza Erans, alias Beef Steak Pete," *Evening Post*, August 24, 1846, both available via the American Antiquarian Society.

13 Quoted in Jonathan Ned Katz, *Gay American History: Lesbians and Gay Men in the U.S.A.* (New York: Plume, 1992), 228.

14 Gilfoyle, *City of Eros*, 136.

15 Tavia Nyong'o, *The Amalgamation Waltz: Race, Performance, and the Ruses of Memory* (Minneapolis: University of Minnesota Press, 2009), 98–9.

16 Ibid., 99.

17 Many of these narratives fell under the genre of "forced feminization," "petticoat punishment," and "mistress" scenarios: stories in which being forced into girls' clothing as a punishment by an older woman or authority figure led the latter to declare that the writers should remain a girl because she simply looked too pretty to be male. Many of the autobiographical forms of these narratives were eroticized. Among self-identified transvestites in the early to mid-twentieth century, role-playing correspondence was also a common iteration of the genre. They have in common the conceit that beginning to dress and live as a woman was an event imposed from the outside on the subject, to rationalize it. See, for an example of the former, the autobiographical story of "Bessie's" forced feminization by a bully at age sixteen in David Cauldwell, ed., *Transvestists Tell Their Stories: Confessions of Person Who Prefer to Dress Like the Opposite Sex* (Girard, KS: Haldeman-Julius Publications, 1947), 9, available at Louise Lawrence Transgender Archive, Vallejo, CA. For an example of stories written through correspondence, see Louise Lawrence's extensive forced-feminization letters and drawings in the Louise Lawrence Collection, Box 1, Series 1B, Folder 6, Kinsey Institute, Bloomington, IN.

18 Saidiya Hartman, "Venus in Two Acts," *Small Axe* 12, no. 2 (2008): 1–14. Marisa Fuentes, *Dispossessed Lives: Enslaved Women, Violence, and the Archive* (Philadelphia: University of Pennsylvania Press, 2016), was especially instructive for critically imagining how Mary Jones may have moved through New Orleans.

19 On gradual emancipation and the ways many enslaved New Yorkers purchased or negotiated their freedom, see White, *Stories of Black Freedom*, 13.

20 White, *Stories of Black Freedom*, 24–31. See also Leslie M. Harris, *In the Shadow of Slavery: African Americans in New York City, 1626–1863* (Chicago: University of Chicago Press, 2003).

21 White, *Stories of Black Freedom*, 45, 52–6, 98–9, 104–5.

22 On the context of the 1834 riots, see Harris, *In the Shadow*, 194–7.

23 See Christine Stansell, *City of Women: Sex and Class in New York, 1789–1860* (Champaign, IL: University of Illinois Press, 1987). However, crucially, Stansell doesn't include the free Black community in this study, a point taken up by Harris in *In the Shadow*, 3.

24 Gilfoyle, *City of Eros*, 30–5.

25 There is a vast literature on the cult of true womanhood, domesticity, and separate-spheres ideology. For a reflective account on the feminist historiography indebted to Barbara Welter's 1966 article "The Cult of True Womanhood, 1820–1860," see Mary Louise Roberts, "True Womanhood Revisited," *Journal of Women's History* 14, no. 1 (2002): 150–5. For a book-length study, see Mary Poovey, *Uneven Developments: The Ideological Work of Gender in Mid-Victorian England* (Chicago: University of Chicago Press, 1988).

26 Hill, *Their Sisters' Keepers*, 82–5, 88–9.

27 Patricia Cline Cohen, Timothy J. Gilfoyle, and Helen Lefkowitz Horowitz, *The Flash Press: Sporting Male Weeklies in 1840s New York* (Chicago: University of Chicago Press, 2008), 1–9.

28 Cohen, Gilfoyle, and Horowitz, *The Flash Press*, 23, 192, 196.

29 Quoted in Katz, *Love Stories*, 50.

30 Cohen, Gilfoyle, and Horowitz, *The Flash Press*, 45.

31 C. J. S. Thompson, *The Mysteries of Sex: Women Who Posed as Men and Men Who Impersonated Women* (London: Hutchinson & Co, 1939), 199–200.

32 Silvia Federici, *Caliban and the Witch: Women, the Body, and Primitive Accumulation* (Brooklyn, NY: Autonomedia, 2004).

33 I am drawing here on John D'Emilio, "Capitalism and Gay Identity," in *The Lesbian and Gay Studies Reader*, ed. Henry Ablelove, Michele Aina Barale, and David M. Halperin (New York: Routledge, 1993), 467–76. See also Christopher Chitty, *Sexual Hegemony: Statecraft, Sodomy, and Capital in the Rise of the World System*, ed. Max Fox (Durham, NC: Duke University Press, 2020).

34 W. E. B. Du Bois, "Of the Black Belt," in *The Souls of Black Folk: Essays and Sketches* (Chicago: A. C. McClurg & Co., 1903), 110–34.

35 John Bardes, "Sailing While Black," 64 *Parishes*, 64parishes.org.

36 Nathalie Dessens, *Creole City: A Chronical of Early American New Orleans* (Gainesville: University of Florida Press, 2015), 151; Kimberly S. Hanger, *Bounded Lives, Bounded Places: Free Black Society in Colonial New Orleans, 1769–1803* (Durham, NC: Duke University Press, 1997), 165–9; and Thomas C. Buchanan, *Black Life on the Mississippi: Slaves, Free Blacks, and the Western Steamboat World* (Chapel Hill: University of North Carolina Press, 2004), 28.

37 Hanger, *Bounded Lives*, 165; Buchanan, *Black Life*, 198n85.

38 E. Douglas Branch, "Success to the Railroad," *Western Pennsylvanian Historical Magazine*, March 1937, 1–14.

39 For greater context about *libres* and the emigrant class from Saint Domingue, see Hanger, *Bounded Lives*, 2–11; and Walter Johnson, *River of Dark Dreams: Slavery and Empire in the Cotton Kingdom* (Cambridge, MA: Harvard University Press, 2013), 33. On 41, Johnson refers to the million enslaved people forcibly relocated to the Mississippi valley.

40 Bardes, "Sailing While Black."

41 John, *River of Dark Dreams*, 215.

42 For a political economic account, see Scott P. Marier, *The Merchant's Capital: New Orleans and the Political Economy of the Nineteenth Century South* (Cambridge, UK: Cambridge University Press, 2013).

43 Hortense J. Spillers, "Mama's Baby, Papa's Maybe: An American Grammar Book," *Diacritics* 17, no. 2 (1987): 67.

44 Ibid., 72.

45 Jennifer L. Morgan, *Laboring Women: Reproduction and Gender in New World Slavery* (Philadelphia: University of Pennsylvania Press, 2004), 56–66, 212–13n96.

46 C. Riley Snorton, *Black on Both Sides: A Racial History of Trans Identity*, 3rd ed. (Minneapolis: University of Minnesota Press, 2017), 57.

47 Ibid., 59, emphasis added.

48 Quoted in ibid., 64–5.

49 See Daniel H. Usner Jr., *American Indians in Early New Orleans: From Calumet to Raquette* (Baton Rouge: Louisiana State University Press, 2018).

50 Dessens, *Creole City*, 76–9.

51 Buchanan, *Black Life*, 30–1.

52 Emily Clark, *The Strange History of the American Quadroon: Free Women of Color in the Revolutionary Atlantic World* (Chapel Hill: University of North Carolina Press, 2013), 170–3.

53 Judith Kelleher Schafer, *Brothels, Depravity, and Abandoned Women: Illegal Sex in Antebellum New Orleans* (Baton Rouge: Louisiana State University Press, 2009), 12, 17, 26, 60.

54 Ibid., 15, 21–2.

55 "Singular Case—An Oath of Allegiance between Two Noted Characters—Love Correspondence, &c.," *New York Herald*, December 21, 1844.

56 US Census Bureau, 1850 Census, Statistics of New York, Population by Counties, 91, 109, https://www2.census.gov/library/publications/decennial/1850/1850a/1850a-22.pdf.

57 David Levine, "African American History: A Past Rooted in the Hudson Valley," *Hudson Valley Magazine*, February 16, 2022, hvmag.com.

58 Snorton, *Black on Both Sides*, 56.

59 See Christina Sharpe, *In the Wake: On Blackness and Being* (Durham, NC: Duke University Pres, 2016).

3. Queens of the Gay World

1 John Rechy, *City of Night*, rev. ed. (New York: Grove Press, 2013).

2 One important romantic treatment of the literary gay outlaw is Leo Bersani's essay on Jean Genet, "The Gay Outlaw," *diacritics* 24, nos. 2–3 (1994): 5–18. Kadji Amin offers a critical response to such idealizations of gay anti-sociality, particularly in reference to Genet, in *Disturbing Attachments: Genet, Modern Pederasty, and Queer History* (Durham, NC: Duke University Press, 2017).

3 "The Fabulous Miss Destiny," *ONE Magazine*, September 1964, available at ONE National Gay and Lesbian Archives, Los Angeles. Rechy claimed in a 1984 essay that she thanked him for portraying her so grandiosely. John Rechy, "City of Night Remembered" (1984), in *Beneath the Skin: The Collected Essays of John Rechy* (Cambridge, MA: De Capo Press, 2009): "I ran into her on Hollywood Boulevard. She gushed 'I want to thank you, my dear, for making me even more famous.' Later she gave a mean interview about me to *One* magazine, which featured her on the cover. Still, I was glad she was getting attention ... I assume she's gone to Heaven, where she shines among queenly angels" (122).

4 Rechy, *City of Night*, 122.

5 For example, the LGB Alliance in Britain is organized through an identification with "lesbian" and "gay" to authorize and pursue anti-trans political goals. For that reason, its charity status is currently under investigation. Samantha Riedel, "LGB Alliance, a British Anti-Trans Organization, Could Lose Its Charity Status," *Them*, September 9, 2022, them.us.

6 Esther Newton, *My Butch Career: A Memoir* (Durham, NC: Duke University Press, 2018), 104.

7 Ibid., 108.

8 Ibid., 113.

9 Esther Newton, *Mother Camp: Female Impersonators in America*, 2nd ed. (Chicago: University of Chicago Press, 1979), 113–14.

10 Ibid., 3.

11 Ibid., 7.

12 Ibid., 8.

13 Ibid.
14 Ibid., 10.
15 Ibid., 18.
16 Ibid., 12.
17 Ibid.
18 Ibid., 14.
19 Ibid., 15.
20 Susan Stryker, *Transgender History: The Roots of Today's Revolution*, 2nd ed. (Boston: Seal Press, 2017), 64–5.
21 Ibid., 61.
22 Newton, *Mother Camp*, 18–19.
23 Ibid., xii.
24 For more on the declassification of homosexuality as a mental disorder, see David Valentine, *Imagining Transgender: An Ethnography of a Category* (Durham, NC: Duke University Press, 2007), 54–7.
25 Newton, *Mother Camp*, xiii n4.
26 Ibid., xii n3.
27 On the various difficulties of navigating the transsexual medical regime, see Joanne Meyerowitz, *How Sex Changed: A History of Transsexuality in the United States* (Cambridge, MA: Harvard University Press, 2004); Stryker, *Transgender History*; Jules Gill-Peterson, *Histories of the Transgender Child* (Minneapolis: University of Minnesota Press, 2018); and C. Riley Snorton, *Black on Both Sides: A Racial History of Trans Identity* (Minneapolis: University of Minnesota Press, 2017).
28 Quoted in Morgan Artyukhina, "'Our Armies Are Rising': Sylvia Rivera and Marsha P. Johnson," *Liberation School*, October 13, 2020, liberationschool.org.
29 The original statement was reprinted by the artist and activist Tourmaline, who has made available a wealth of archival materials upon which this chapter relies. "NYU Occupation: Street Transvestites for Gay Power Statement, October 1970," *The Spirit Was*, February 22, 2013, thespiritwas.tumblr.com.
30 Quoted in Jessi Gan, "'Still at the Back of the Bus': Sylvia Rivera's Struggle," *Centro Journal* 19, no. 1 (2007): 129.
31 "Sylvia Rivera and Marsha P. Johnson: Listen to the Newly Unearthed Interview with Street Transvestite Action Revolutionaries," New York City Historical Society, June 26, 2019, nyhistory.org.
32 Quoted in ibid.
33 On the complex emergence of anti-trans lesbian politics, see Finn Enke, "Collective Memory and the Transfeminist 1970s: Toward a Less Plausible History," *TSQ: Transgender Studies Quarterly* 5, no. 1 (2018): 9–29.

NOTES FROM PAGES 113 TO 125

34 Although it was removed from *Vimeo*, where Tourmaline uploaded the footage, the video remains accessible in multiple other places online at the time of this writing. @tourmaline, "this week vimeo took down the Sylvia Rivera 'y'all better quiet down' speech I uploaded in 2012 b/c of 'copyright issues,'" *Twitter*, April 17, 2017, twitter.com.

35 Accounts of We'wha's visit to Washington, DC, are unfortunately mediated by white authorship. See Eliza McFeely, *Zuni and the American Imagination* (New York: Hill & Wang, 2001), 44–65; and Will Roscoe, *The Zuni Man-Woman* (Albuquerque: University of New Mexico Press, 1992).

36 Rechy, *City of Night*, 131.

37 In truth, the gendered difference between a king and a queen was also significant when the power invested in the crown had long been associated with maleness. When Elizabeth I took the throne, a woman sovereign was no longer a philosophical hypothetical but a practical matter. Although the crown could sit atop the head of any mortal body, could a woman wield the power of the king without becoming herself masculine? Some critics were convinced during Elizabeth's rule that she must secretly possess a penis, for nothing else could explain her capacity to rule like a king. The street queen, no doubt, inherited and had to work out such matters to an even more intense degree, since the admixture of masculine and feminine were encoded in her even more literally. See Carole Levin, *The Reign and Life of Queen Elizabeth I: Queenship and Power* (London: Palgrave Macmillan, 2022), 241–58. I want to thank Margaret Speer for sharing this controversy over Elizabeth's sex with me.

38 Quoted in Ernst Kantorowicz, *The King's Two Bodies: A Study in Medieval Political Theology* (Princeton, NJ: Princeton University Press, 2016), 13.

39 Ibid.,10–11.

40 Rechy, *City of Night*, 132.

41 Ibid., 134.

42 Ibid., 141.

43 Ibid., 142.

44 Ibid., 138.

45 Ibid., 143.

46 Ibid.

47 Sarah McBride, "Fifty Years after Stonewall, HRC Commemorates the Riots That Helped Spark a Movement," Human Rights Campaign, June 28, 2019, hrc.org. For an example of linking Sylvia Rivera directly to same-sex marriage, see Eric Cervini, "Why We Owe LGBTQ+ Victories to an Early Trans Activist," *Time*, June

30, 2020, time.com. On the corporate hagiography of Salesforce, see Isabel Goncalves, "Honoring Trailblazers Who Paved the Way for the LGBTQ Movement," *Salesforce 360 Blog*, June 19, 2019, salesforce.com.

48 Judith Butler, *Bodies That Matter: On the Discursive Limits of Sex* (New York: Routledge, 2011), 88.

49 Ibid., 90: "In the pursuit of realness this subject is produced, a phantasmatic pursuit that mobilizes identifications, underscoring the phantasmatic promise that constitutes an identificatory move —a promise which, taken too seriously, can culminate only in disappointment and disidentification. A fantasy that for Venus, because she dies—killed apparently by one of her clients, perhaps after the discovery of those remaining organs—cannot be translated into the symbolic. This is a killing that is performed by a symbolic that would eradicate those phenomena that require an opening up of the possibilities for the resignification of sex. If Venus wants to become a woman, and cannot overcome being a Latina, then Venus is treated by the symbolic precisely the ways in which women of color are treated. Her death thus testifies to a tragic misreading of the social map of power."

50 Ibid., 90.

51 Jay Prosser, *Second Skins* (New York: Columbia University Press, 1998); Viviane Namaste, *Invisible Lives: The Erasure of Transsexual and Transgendered People* (Chicago: University of Chicago Press, 2000).

52 Walker Caplan, "*The Guardian* Published a Judith Butler Interview—and Then Deleted an Answer about TERFS," *Lithub*, September 9, 2021, lithub.com.

53 Butler, *Bodies That Matter*, 89

54 bell hooks, "Is Paris Burning?," in *Black Looks: Race and Representation*, 2nd ed. (New York: Routledge, 2015), 146–56.

55 C. Riley Snorton and Jin Haritaworn, "Trans Necropolitics: A Transnational Reflection on Violence, Death, and the Trans of Color Afterlife," in *Transgender Studies Reader*, vol. 2, ed. Susan Stryker and Aren Aizura (New York: Routledge, 2012).

56 Roderick A. Ferguson, *Aberrations in Black: Toward a Queer of Color Critique* (Minneapolis: University of Minnesota Press, 2003), 2.

57 Ibid., 23, emphasis added: "As the site of nonheteronormative difference, African American culture materially and discursively registers the gender and sexual homogeneity of African American racial formations *as critiques* of the contradictions of state and capital and the regulations of canonical sociology."

58 Lyle Harris and Marlon Riggs, "Revolutionary Acts—Interview with Marlon Riggs," *Afterimage* 18 (1991): 9. I thank Anthony

M. Petro for getting me a copy of this interview after I had stalled out several times in my research efforts.

59 Essex Hemphill, "Homocide: For Ronald Gibson (1982)," *Victor Yates* (blog), May 19, 2011, victoryates.wordpress.com.
60 Harris and Riggs, "Revolutionary Acts," 10.
61 Rechy, *City of Night*, 144.

Conclusion

1 Janice Raymond, *The Transsexual Empire: The Making of the She Male* (Boston: Beacon Press, 1979).
2 Kathleen Stock, "Can Biological Males Be Lesbians?," *Article*, May 10, 2019, thearticle.com.
3 Abigail Shrier, *Irreversible Damage: The Transgender Craze Seducing Our Daughters* (Washington, DC: Regenery Press, 2020), 39.
4 Andrew R. Flores et al, "Gender Identity Disparities in Criminal Victimization," Williams Institute, University of California, Los Angeles, March 2021, williamsinstitute.law.ucla.edu.
5 W. Carsten Andresen, "Research Note: Comparing the Gay and Trans Panic Defense," *Women and Criminal Justice* 32, nos. 1–2 (August 2021), 219–41. See also Gayle Salamon, *The Life and Death of Latisha King: A Critical Phenomenology of Transphobia* (New York: NYU Press, 2018).
6 Women's Human Rights Campaign (WHRC) UK, "Submission to Women and Equalities Committee on Reform of the Gender Recognition Act," November 27, 2020, available at committees. parliament.uk, 6. See also Vic Parsons, "MPs Urged by Anti-Trans 'Women's Rights' Group to Eliminate 'Transgenderism' and Scrap Gender Recognition Act," *Pink News*, January 27, 2021, pinknews. co.uk.
7 @jk_rowling, "Safeguarding exists not because all members of a group are a threat to another group, but because sufficient are to justify protected spaces for the more vulnerable group. Trans women retain the same pattern of sex offending/violence as males," September 16, 2022, twitter.com.
8 Alexander Kacla, "After Violent Threats, Family of Transgender Girl Looks to Leave Town," NBC News, August 20, 2018, nbcnews.com.
9 Jay Root, "Texas GOP Candidate Shelly Luther Complains That Students Can't Make Fun of Transgender Children," *Houston Chronicle*, February 9, 2022, houstonchronicle.com.
10 Kacla, "Violent Threats."
11 Devan Cole, "Arkansas Becomes First States to Outlaw Gender-

Affirming Treatment for Trans Youth," CNN, April 6, 2021, cnn. com; Devan Cole, Juliana Battaglioa, and Konstantin Toropin, "Mississippi Governor Signs Bill Banning Transgender Students from Women's Sports, Approving First Anti-trans Law of 2021," CNN, March 11, 2021, cnn.com; S.B. No. 1646, "A Bill to be Entitled an Act Relating to the Definition of Abuse of a Child," Texas Senate, filed March 11, 2021, available at capitol.texas.gov. See also Megan Munce, "Gender-Affirming Medical Treatment for Transgender Kids Would Be Considered Child Abuse under Texas Senate Bill," *Texas Tribune*, April 27, 2021, texastribune.org.

12 One of the most disturbing examples of this was right-wing media suggestions that a school shooter in Nashville who may have identified as trans masculine or nonbinary was a trans woman, as if that explained the extreme violence. Brendan Smialowski, "Some on the Right Blame Gender Identity and Not Guns for Nashville Shooting," *NBC News*, March 28, 2023, nbcnews.com.

13 For a longer treatment of the laundering of extremism by anti-trans pundits, see Jules Gill-Peterson, "From Gender Critical to QAnon: Anti-trans Politics and the Laundering of Conspiracy," *New Inquiry*, September 13, 2021, thenewinquiry.com.

14 Graeme Massie, "Jordan Peterson: Anger as Joe Rogan Guest Says Being Trans Is 'Contagion' Similar to 'Satanic Ritual Abuse,'" *Independent*, January 27, 2022, independent.co.uk. The anti-Semitic reproduction of conspiracy theories about fabulated Jewish funding of trans causes became a major point of contention over Helen Joyce's book *Trans: When Ideology Meets Reality* (New York: Simon & Schuster, 2021).

15 Natasha Frost, "Australian State Moves to Ban Nazi Salute after Clashes at Rally," *New York Times*, March 20, 2023, nytimes.com.

16 Sonia Correa, David Patternotte, and Roman Kuhar, "The Globalisation of Anti-gender Campaigns," *International Politics and Society*, May 31, 2018, ips-journal.eu; "India's Transgender Protestors Fear Stateless Future, *France 24*, March 12, 2019, france24. com; Scott Neuman, "Local Governments in Poland Rescind Anti-LGBT Resolutions, Fearing Loss of EU Funding," NPR, September 28, 2021, npr.org; Zack Beauchamp, "How Hatred of Gay People Became a Key Plank in Hungary's Authoritarian Turn," *Vox*, June 28, 2021, vox.com; Jennifer Ann Thomas, "Threats against Trans Councilwoman Stir Violence Fears in Brazil," *Reuters*, February 5, 2021, reuters.com; "Philippines President Pardons US Marine in Transgender Killing," *France 24*, July 9, 2020, france24.com; Viktoria Serdult, "Tucker Carlson Has Become Obsessed with Hungary. Here's What He Doesn't Understand," *Politico*, January 2, 2022, politico.com; Maite Fernandez Simon, "'A Woman Is a

Woman, a Man Is a Man': Putin Compares Gender Nonconformity to the Coronavirus Pandemic," *Washington Post*, December 23, 2021, washingtonpost.com; and Nick Duffy, "Council of Europe Condemns 'virulent attacks on LGBT rights' in the UK, Hungary, and Poland," *iNews*, January 25, 2022, inews.co.uk.

17 For an overview of the scientific rejection of autogynephilia, see Julia Serano, "Autogynephilia: A Scientific Review, Feminist Analysis, and Alternative 'Embodiment Fantasies' Model," *Sociological Review* 68, no. 4 (2020): 763–78.

18 "Trans Men Fight Back," Gender Dysphoria Alliance Canada, July 24, 2021. The original post on the GDAC official website has been taken down but is available at web.archive.org/web/20210724122022/https://www.gdalliancecanada.com/post/trans-men-fight-back.

19 Jo Yurcaba, "Caitlyn Jenner Says Transgender Girls in Women's Sports Is 'Unfair,'" NBC News, May 3, 2021, nbcnews.com.

20 Adia María Isasi-Díaz, *Mujerista Theology: A Theology for the Twenty-First Century* (Ossining, NY: Orbis Books, 1996).

21 Don Kulick, *Travesti: Sex, Gender, and Culture among Brazilian Transgendered Prostitutes* (Chicago: University of Chicago Press, 1998), 91.

22 Mariana Fernández Camacho, "Treinta años de transfeminismo en Argentina," *El Salto*, August 10, 2020, elsaltodiario.com.

23 On travesti history in Spain, see Iñaki Estella, "The Collective Scene: Transvestite Cabaret during the End of Francoist Spain," *TSQ: Transgender Studies Quarterly* 8, no. 4 (2021): 498–515; for an important decolonial and Indigenous reading of travesti ways of life in the Canary Islands, see Daniasa Curbelo, "The Ohters of the Ravine," *TSQ: Transgender Studies Quarterly* 8, no. 4 (2021): 481–97. In France, *travesti* was a common term on the gay left in the 1970s, though interestingly it is increasingly being scrubbed from historical memory. The recent translation and reissue of Guy Hocquenghem's *Gay Liberation after May '68* (Durham: Duke University Press, 2022), first published in 1974, included a decision to translate "travesti" as "trans" and "transgender," despite the many potential inaccuracies of doing so.

24 See Kulick, *Travesti*, for an overview.

25 Dora Silva Santana, "Mais Viva!: Reassembling Transness, Blackness, and Feminism," *TSQ: Transgender Studies Quarterly* 6, no. 2 (2019): 210–22; Giancarlo Fernando Cornejo Salinas, "Travesti Memory and Politics: Toward a Peruvian Transgender Imaginary," PhD diss., University of California-Berkeley, 2018. For an overview of "travesti" and its relationships to "trans," see Cole

Rizki, "Latin/x American Trans Studies: Toward a Travesti-Trans Analytic," *TSQ: Transgender Studies Quarterly* 6, no. 2 (2019): 145–55.

26 Maria Ochoa, *Queen for a Day: Transformistas, Beauty Queens, and the Performances of Femininity in Venezuela* (Durham, NC: Duke University Press, 2014).

27 Malú Machuco Rose, "Giuseppe Campuzano's Afterlife: Toward a Travesti Methodology for Critique, Care, and Radical Resistance," *TSQ: Transgender Studies Quarterly* 6, no. 2 (2019): 242–3.

28 Hillary Hiner, Juan Carlos Garrido, and Brigette Walters, "Anti-trans State Terrorism: Trans and Travesti Women, Human Rights, and Recent History in Chile," *TSQ: Transgender Studies Quarterly* 6, no. 2 (2019): 201.

29 Santana, "Mais Viva!," 212.

30 Rose, "Giuseppe Campuzano's Afterlife," 242.

31 "The Yogyakarta Principles," English ed., 2006, yogyakarta principles.org.

32 Martín De Mauro Rucovsky and Ian Russell, "The Travesti Critique of the Gender Identity Law in Argentina," *TSQ: Transgender Studies Quarterly* 6, no. 2 (2019): 223–38.

33 Quoted in ibid., 231.

34 Marlene Wayar, *Travesti: Una teoría lo suficientemente buena* (Buenos Aires: Muchas Nueces, 2019), 18.

35 Ibid., 99. My translation.

36 Ibid., 104. My translation.

37 Linn da Quebrada, "Mulher," YouTube video, April 14, 2017, youtube.com.

38 Santana, "Mais Viva!," 215, emphasis added.

Index

projected onto rest of
world, 14
as fitting well into larger
concept of misogyny,
142–3
as fracturing political
solidarity of gay liberation
banner, 114
fraudulence of, 142
as mode of colonial statecraft,
15
as part of larger state-
sponsored pattern of
violence, 54
resilience of, 137
use of term, vii, 26–7
trans panic
blending of state violence with
interpersonal violence as
signature outcome of global
trans panic, 48
as blurring into homophobia
and gay panic, 47–8
emergence of, 29–30, 36
first person account of, 41
as global, 21, 22, 29–59, 116
in India, 30, 35–6
intimacy of with gay panic,
143
as marking populations as
trans feminine, or trans-
feminizing them, 31
as not merely expression of
individual hatred, 55
as phenomenon with global
reach, 48
as recognizable form of state
violence, 21, 31
retaliatory violence of, 55
TERFs as having own version
of, 24
treatment of by psychology, 11
use of by colonial states as
pretense to secure political
and economic power, 37

trans panic defense, 6, 7–8, 21,
50, 54, 137, 138
transsexual, as new kind of trans
woman, 108
trans tipping point, 4
trans womanhood
relationship of with public
space and economic
mobility, 79
as strangely unthinkable, 135,
136
as strongly associated with sex
work, 22, 59
as tracking with historical
changes in state power and
political economy, 92
trans misogyny as exceeding,
56
use of term, 18
trans women
Black trans women, 3–5, 18,
22, 53, 58, 59, 70, 91, 94,
124–31
coherent history of as
not possible or worth
attempting, 16
of color, 124–31
as extra, 141
extreme criminalization of
Black trans women, 53
history of, 75
killing of by men, 8, 38
Mary Jones as early example
of modern Black trans
women's history, 70
as not discrete, separate group
of people, 142
as not intrinsically inviting
reprisal, 11
place of poor ones in LBGT
movement, 101
as sex workers, 57–8
transsexual as new kind of,
108
use of term, 18